Property Maintenance Code
of New York State

New York State
Department of State
Division of Code Enforcement and Administration

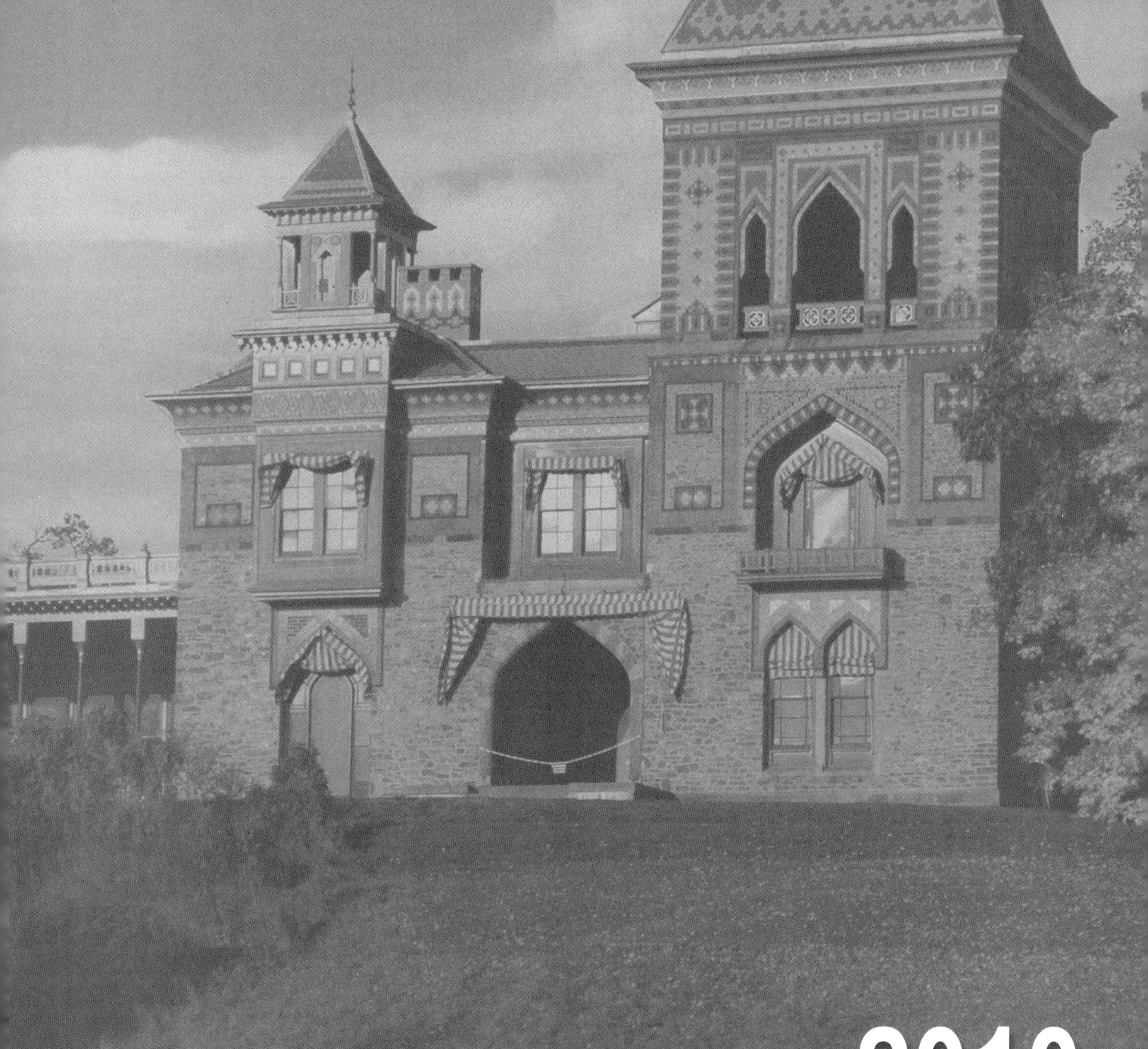

2010

David A. Paterson Governor
Lorraine Cortés-Vázquez Secretary of State

2010 Property Maintenance Code of New York State

Publication Date: August 2010

ISBN: 978-1-60983-007-6

COPYRIGHT © 2010
by

International Code Council, Inc.
500 New Jersey Avenue, NW, 6th Floor
Washington, D.C. 20001

and

New York State
Department of State
99 Washington Avenue
Albany, NY 12231

Cover Photo Credits: Courtesy of New York State Office of Parks, Recreation and Historic Preservation.

Darwin Martin House State Historic Site: The Darwin Martin House, located in Buffalo, New York, is one of Frank Lloyd Wright's most celebrated Prairie style homes. Constructed for the Martin family in the early 1900s, the house features Wright's signature low, horizontal design and free-flowing plan. This National Historic Landmark property, which includes several interconnected buildings and landscape features, is being meticulously restored to its 1907 appearance.

Olana State Historic Site: Olana, located in Hudson, New York, is the spectacular 19th-century estate of Hudson River School painter Frederic Edwin Church. The magnificent Persian style house and studio as well as the surrounding landscape were designed by Church. The property, a National Historic Landmark, offers dramatic views of the Hudson Valley that inspired Church's paintings.

ALL RIGHTS RESERVED. This work contains (1) portions of the International Code Council Codes (the "ICC Codes") and (2) material that is derivative of the ICC Codes, and (3) wholly original materials prepared by the New York State Department of State or by the New York State Fire Prevention and Building Code Council (the "Code Council"). The International Code Council has copyright ownership of the ICC Codes. The International Code Council and the New York State Department of State have joint copyright ownership of the material that is derivative of the ICC Codes. The New York State Department of State has copyright ownership of the wholly original materials prepared by the New York State Department of State or by the Code Council. As to the ICC Codes, all rights, including the right of reproduction in whole or in part in any form, are reserved to the International Code Council. As to the material that is derivative of the ICC Codes, all rights, including the right of reproduction in whole or in part in any form, are reserved to the International Code Council and the New York State Department of State, jointly. As to the wholly original materials prepared by the New York State Department of State or by the Code Council, all rights, including the right of reproduction in whole or in part in any form, are reserved to the New York State Department of State. For information on permission to copy material exceeding fair use, please contact: International Code Council, Publications, 4051 West Flossmoor Road, Country Club Hills, IL 60478 (Phone 888-422-7233).

Trademarks: "International Code Council," the "International Code Council" logo and the "International Property Maintenance Code" are trademarks of the International Code Council, Inc.

PRINTED IN THE U.S.A.

ACKNOWLEDGMENTS

The Department of State gratefully acknowledges the following individuals who contributed to the development of the *Property Maintenance Code of New York State*:

STATE FIRE PREVENTION AND BUILDING CODE COUNCIL

Lorraine A. Cortés-Vázquez	Chair - Secretary of State, NYS Department of State
Ronald E. Piester, AIA	designee - Director, NYS Department of State Division of Code Enforcement & Administration
Floyd Madison	State Fire Administrator - NYS Office of Fire Prevention & Control
John F. Mueller	designee - Deputy State Fire Administrator NYS. Office of Fire Prevention & Control
Richard F. Daines, M.D.	Commissioner - NYS Department of Health
Richard W. Svenson, P.E.	designee - Director, NYS Department of Health Division of Environmental Health Protection
M. Patricia Smith	Commissioner - NYS Department of Labor
Blaise Thomas, P.E.	designee - NYS Department of Labor Associate Engineer, Engineering Services
Michael R. Bloomberg	Mayor - City of New York
John H. Lee, R.A.	designee - New York City Buildings
Matthew J. Driscoll	Mayor - City of Syracuse
Nicholas Altieri	designee - City of Syracuse, Code Enforcement Inspection Office
Randolph F. Bateman	Mayor - City of Oswego
Neal Smith	designee - Director of Code Enforcement
Michael W. Behling	Legislator - County of Jefferson
David Ross	designee - Code Enforcement Official
Robert E. Olson	Councilman - Town of Horicon
L. Stephen Brescia	Mayor - Village of Montgomery
Carmen R. Dubaldi, Jr.	designee - Orange County, Division of Risk Management
Joseph F. Sauerwein	Fire Service Official Blue Point Fire District
Gary B. Higbee, AIA	Registered Architect - Director of Industry Development The Steel Institute of New York
Thomas B. Vanderbeek, P.E.	Professional Engineer
John H. Flanigan	Code Enforcement Official
Robert Hankin	Builders' Representative
John J. Torpey	Trade Union Representative
Richard M. Vargas	Persons with Disabilities Representative NYS Commission on Quality of Care and Advocacy for Persons with Disabilities

DEPARTMENT OF STATE

Lorraine A. Cortés-Vázquez	Secretary of State
Daniel Shapiro	First Deputy Secretary of State
Ronald E. Piester, AIA	Director - Division of Code Enforcement & Administration
Thomas P. Mahar	Deputy Director - Division of Code Enforcement & Administration
Raymond J. Andrews, R.A.	Assistant Director for Code Development - Division of Code Enforcement & Administration
Joseph P. Ball, Esq.	Office of Counsel

PROPERTY MAINTENANCE CODE TECHNICAL SUBCOMMITTEE

Thomas Mahar (Chair), David Hall, P.E., - Department of State Staff
James Morganson, Terry Brennan, James Bailey, James Godfrey, Dennis Penman

Content

The *Property Maintenance Code of New York State* combines language from the 2006 *International Property Maintenance Code®* and New York modifications developed by the State Fire Prevention and Building Code Council and its Property Maintenance Code Technical Subcommittee.

Marginal Markings

Solid vertical lines in the margins within the body of the code indicate a technical change from the requirements of the 2007 Edition. Deletion indicators (➡) are provided in the margin where a paragraph or item has been deleted.

Letter Designations in Front of Section Numbers

The content of sections in this code which begin with a letter designation are maintained by another code development committee in accordance with the following: [B] Building Code; [F] Fire Code; [M] Mechanical Code and [P] Plumbing Code.

TABLE OF CONTENTS

CHAPTER 1 GENERAL REQUIREMENTS........1

Section
- 101 Title, Scope and Purpose 1
- 102 Applicability.............................1
- 103 Materials, Equipment and Methods of Construction 2
- 104 Service Utilities 2
- 105 Temporary Structures.....................2
- 106 Maintenance of Equipment and Systems 2
- 107 Unsafe Structures and Equipment 3
- 108 Emergency Measures 3
- 109 Administration and Enforcement 3

CHAPTER 2 DEFINITIONS 5

Section
- 201 General................................5
- 202 General Definitions 5

CHAPTER 3 GENERAL REQUIREMENTS........7

Section
- 301 General................................7
- 302 Exterior Property Areas 7
- 303 Swimming Pools, Spas and Hot Tubs 8
- 304 Exterior Structure........................9
- 305 Interior Structure 10
- 306 Handrails and Guardrails 11
- 307 Rubbish and Garbage 11
- 308 Extermination..........................11

CHAPTER 4 LIGHT, VENTILATION AND OCCUPANCY LIMITATIONS 13

Section
- 401 General...............................13
- 402 Light 13
- 403 Ventilation 13
- 404 Occupancy Limitations...................13

CHAPTER 5 PLUMBING FACILITIES AND FIXTURE REQUIREMENTS........17

Section
- 501 General...............................17
- 502 Required Facilities 17
- 503 Toilet Rooms 17
- 504 Plumbing Systems and Fixtures.............17
- 505 Water System..........................17
- 506 Sanitary Drainage System 18
- 507 Storm Drainage 18

CHAPTER 6 MECHANICAL AND ELECTRICAL REQUIREMENTS.................19

Section
- 601 General...............................19
- 602 Heating Facilities 19
- 603 Mechanical Equipment 19
- 604 Electrical Facilities......................19
- 605 Electrical Equipment 20
- 606 Elevators, Escalators and Dumbwaiters........20
- 607 Duct Systems 20
- 608 Assistive Listening Systems................20

CHAPTER 7 FIRE SAFETY REQUIREMENTS.................21

Section
- 701 General...............................21
- 702 Means of Egress........................21
- 703 Fire-resistance Ratings...................21
- 704 Fire Protection Systems 21
- 705 Carbon Monoxide Alarms 22

CHAPTER 8 REFERENCED STANDARDS.......23

INDEX......................................25

CHAPTER 1
GENERAL REQUIREMENTS

SECTION 101
TITLE, SCOPE AND PURPOSE

101.1 Title. These provisions shall be known as the *Property Maintenance Code of New York State* and shall be cited as such and will be referred to herein as "this code."

101.2 Scope. The provisions of this code shall apply to all existing residential and nonresidential structures and all existing premises and constitute minimum requirements and standards for premises, structures, equipment and facilities for light, ventilation, space, heating, sanitation, protection from the elements, life safety, safety from fire and other hazards, and for safe and sanitary maintenance; the responsibility of owners, operators and occupants; the occupancy of existing structures and premises.

101.3 Purpose. This code is intended to provide minimum requirements to safeguard public safety, health and general welfare insofar as they are affected by the occupancy and maintenance of structures and premises.

SECTION 102
APPLICABILITY

102.1 General. Where, in any specific case, different sections of this code specify different materials, methods of construction or other requirements, the most restrictive shall be applicable. Where there is a conflict between a general requirement and a specific requirement, the specific requirement shall be applicable.

102.2 Other laws and regulations. This code is part of the State Uniform Fire Prevention and Building Code (the Uniform Code) promulgated pursuant to Article 18 of the Executive Law. The provisions of the Uniform Code shall not be deemed to nullify any federal, state or local law, ordinance, administrative code, rule or regulation relating to any matter as to which the Uniform Code does not provide. However:

(1) Pursuant to Section 383(1) of the Executive Law, and except as otherwise provided in paragraphs a, b and c of Section 383 of the Executive Law, the provisions of the Uniform Code supersede any other provision of a general, special or local law, ordinance, administrative code, rule or regulation inconsistent or in conflict with the Uniform Code;

(2) Pursuant to Section 379(3) of the Executive Law, no city, town, village, county or other municipality shall have the power to supersede, void, repeal, or make less restrictive any provision of the Uniform Code; and

(3) The ability of any city, town, or village, or the County of Nassau, to enact or adopt, and to enforce, a local law or ordinance imposing higher or more restrictive standards for construction within the jurisdiction of such city, town, village, or county than are applicable generally to such city, town, village, or county in the Uniform Code is subject to the provisions and requirements of Section 379 of the Executive Law.

Nothing in this Section 102.2 shall be construed (1) as affecting the authority of the State Labor Department to enforce a safety or health standard issued under provisions of Sections 27 and 27-a of the Labor Law; (2) to relieve a person from complying with a stricter standard issued pursuant to the Occupational Safety and Health Act of 1970, as amended; (3) as superseding, limiting, impairing or otherwise affecting any provision in Parts 1219 to 1228 of Title 19 of the New York Codes, Rules and Regulations, as now in effect and as hereafter amended from time to time.

102.3 Change of use or occupancy. No change shall be made in the use or occupancy of any structure that would place the structure in a different division of the same group or occupancy or in a different group of occupancies, unless such structure is made to comply with the requirements of the *Existing Building Code of New York State*.

102.4 Application of references. References to chapter or section numbers, or to provisions not specifically identified by number, shall be construed to refer to such chapter, section or provision of this code.

102.5 Referenced standards. The standards referenced in this code shall be considered part of the requirements of this code to the prescribed extent of each such reference. Where differences occur between provisions of this code and referenced standards, the provisions of this code shall apply.

102.6 Application of other codes. Repairs, additions or alterations to a structure, or changes of occupancy, shall be done in accordance with the applicable procedures and provisions of the *Residential Code of New York State*, the *Building Code of New York State*, the *Plumbing Code of New York State*, the *Mechanical Code of New York State*, the *Fuel Gas Code of New York State*, the *Fire Code of New York State*, the *Existing Building Code of New York State* or the *Energy Conservation Construction Code of New York State*.

102.7 Partial invalidity. In the event any part or provision of this code is held to be illegal or void, this shall not have the effect of making void or illegal any of the other parts or provisions.

102.8 Existing structures. The legal occupancy of any structure existing on the date of adoption of this code shall be permitted to continue without change, except as is specifically covered in this code, the *Fire Code of New York State* or the *Existing Building Code of New York State*.

SECTION 103
MATERIALS, EQUIPMENT AND METHODS OF CONSTRUCTION

103.1 Approved materials and equipment. Materials, equipment and devices approved by the code enforcement official for use shall be constructed and installed in accordance with such approval. Materials, equipment and devices tested by an approved testing laboratory shall be permitted to be constructed and installed in accordance with such approval.

103.2 Used materials and equipment. Material, equipment and devices shall not be reused unless they meet the requirements of the *Residential Code of New York State*, the *Building Code of New York State*, the *Plumbing Code of New York State*, the *Mechanical Code of New York State*, the *Fuel Gas Code of New York State*, the *Fire Code of New York State*, the *Existing Building Code of New York State,* and the *Energy Conservation Construction Code of New York State* and this code for new materials.

103.3 Alternate materials, design and methods of construction and equipment. This code is not intended to prevent the use of any material not specifically prescribed by this code or to prohibit any design or method of construction not specifically prescribed by this code, provided that any such alternative material, design or method of construction has been approved by the code enforcement official or the State Fire Prevention and Building Code Council. An alternative material, design or method of construction may be approved only when the code enforcement official or the State Fire Prevention and Building Code Council shall have determined, in writing, that such alternative material, design or method of construction (1) complies with the intent of the provisions of this code and (2) is at least the equivalent of that prescribed in this code in quality, strength, effectiveness, fire resistance, durability and safety. Nothing in this Section 103.3 shall be construed as permitting any code enforcement official, or any town, village, city, county, or state agency charged with the administration and enforcement of the Uniform Code, to waive, vary, modify or otherwise alter any provision or requirement of this code or any other provision or requirement of the Uniform Code. Provisions or requirements of the Uniform Code may be varied or modified only pursuant to procedures established by the Secretary of State pursuant to Section 381(1)(f) of the Executive Law.

103.4 Safeguards during construction. All construction work covered in this code, including any demolition, shall comply with the requirements of the *Fire Code of New York State* and Chapter 33 of the *Building Code of New York State*.

103.5 Workmanship. Repairs, maintenance work, alterations or installations which are caused directly or indirectly by the enforcement of this code shall be executed and installed in a workmanlike manner and installed in accordance with this code and the manufacturer's installation instructions.

SECTION 104
SERVICE UTILITIES

104.1 Connection of service utilities. Connections from a utility, source of energy, fuel or power to any building or system which is regulated by this code shall be made in accordance with the regulations of the public utility or other authority having jurisdiction.

104.2 Temporary power. Temporary power shall comply with the requirements of Chapter 27 of the *Building Code of New York State*.

SECTION 105
TEMPORARY STRUCTURES

105.1 Conformance. Temporary structures shall conform to Chapter 31, Section 3103 of the *Building Code of New York State* and Chapter 24 of the *Fire Code of New York State*.

SECTION 106
MAINTENANCE OF EQUIPMENT AND SYSTEMS

106.1 Maintenance. Equipment, systems, devices and safeguards required by this code or a previous regulation or code under which the structure or premises was constructed, altered or repaired shall be maintained in good working order. The requirements of this code are not intended to provide the basis for removal or abrogation of fire protection and safety systems and devices in existing structures. Except as otherwise specified herein, the owner or the owner's designated agent shall be responsible for the maintenance of buildings, structures and premises.

106.2 Existing nonrequired equipment and systems. Whenever or wherever any nonrequired device, equipment, system, condition, arrangement, level of protection or any other feature is provided, such device, equipment, system, condition, arrangement, level of protection or other feature shall thereafter be continuously maintained in accordance with this code and applicable referenced standards.

> **Exception:** Nonrequired devices, equipment and systems are permitted to be removed or disabled as provided herein.
>
> 1. Nonrequired devices, equipment and systems are permitted to be removed in entirety;
> 2. Nonrequired devices, equipment and systems are permitted to be disabled, provided that all visible elements are removed;
> 3. Electrically charged devices, equipment and systems are permitted to be disabled, provided that they are disconnected from power sources and all visible elements are labeled as not being energized; and
> 4. Nonrequired fire protection systems are permitted to be disabled, provided that sprinkler heads, exposed valves, fire department connections, initiating and notification devices and similar equipment are

removed, and any remaining visible components are labeled as not being in service.

SECTION 107
UNSAFE STRUCTURES AND EQUIPMENT

107.1 General. When a structure or equipment is found to be unsafe, or when a structure is found unfit for human occupancy, or is found unlawful, such structure shall be condemned pursuant to the provisions of this code.

107.1.1 Unsafe structures. An unsafe structure is one that is found to be dangerous to the life, health, property or safety of the public or the occupants of the structure by not providing minimum safeguards to protect or warn occupants in the event of fire, or because such structure contains unsafe equipment or is so damaged, decayed, dilapidated, structurally unsafe, or of such faulty construction or unstable foundation, that partial or complete collapse is possible.

107.1.2 Unsafe equipment. Unsafe equipment includes any boiler, heating equipment, elevator, moving stairway, electrical wiring or device, flammable liquid containers or other equipment on the premises or within the structure which is in such disrepair or condition that such equipment is a hazard to life, health, property or safety of the public or occupants of the premises or structure.

107.1.3 Structure unfit for human occupancy. A structure is unfit for human occupancy whenever such structure is unsafe, unlawful or, because of the degree to which the structure is in disrepair or lacks maintenance, is insanitary, vermin or rat infested, contains filth and contamination, or lacks ventilation, illumination, sanitary or heating facilities or other essential equipment required by this code, or because the location of the structure constitutes a hazard to the occupants of the structure or to the public.

107.1.4 Unlawful structure. An unlawful structure is one found in whole or in part to be occupied by more persons than permitted under this code, or was erected, altered or occupied contrary to law.

107.2 Vacant structures. Vacant structures shall comply with Sections F311.1 through F311.5 of the *Fire Code of New York State*.

107.3 Notice. Whenever a structure or equipment has been condemned under the provisions of this section, a notice shall be posted in a conspicuous place in or about the structure affected by such notice. If the notice pertains to equipment, it shall also be placed on the condemned equipment.

107.4 Prohibited occupancy. No person shall occupy a placarded premises or shall operate placarded equipment.

107.5 Placard removal. The placard shall be removed whenever the defect or defects upon which the condemnation and placarding action were based have been eliminated.

SECTION 108
EMERGENCY MEASURES

108.1 Imminent danger. When there is imminent danger of failure or collapse of a building or structure which endangers life, or when any structure or part of a structure has fallen and life is endangered by the occupation of the structure, or when there is actual or potential danger to the building occupants or those in the proximity of any structure because of explosives, explosive fumes or vapors or the presence of toxic fumes, gases or materials, or operation of defective or dangerous equipment, the occupants shall vacate the premises forthwith. There shall be posted at each entrance to such structure a notice reading as follows: "This Structure Is Unsafe and Its Occupancy Has Been Prohibited by the Code Enforcement Official." It shall be unlawful for any person to enter such structure except for the purpose of securing the structure, making the required repairs, removing the hazardous condition or of demolishing the same.

SECTION 109
ADMINISTRATION AND ENFORCEMENT

109.1 Administration and enforcement. Administration and enforcement of the *New York State Uniform Fire Prevention and Building Code* shall be in accordance with local law, subject to the minimum requirements set forth in the "Official Compilation of Codes Rules and Regulations of the State of New York," 19 NYCRR Part 1203, "Minimum Standards for Administration and Enforcement." State agencies shall comply with the minimum requirements set forth in 9 NYCRR Part 1204, "Administration and Enforcement by State Agencies."

109.2 Modification. No town, village, city or county, nor any state agency charged with the administration and enforcement of this code may waive, modify or otherwise alter any provision of this code unless approved by the State Fire Prevention and Building Code Council in accordance with Section 379 of Article 18 of the Executive Law.

109.3 Application for variance or appeal. Variance or appeal of any provision of this code shall be in accordance with the provisions of the "Official Compilation of Codes, Rules and Regulations of the State of New York," 19 NYCRR Part 1205, "Variance Procedures."

CHAPTER 2
DEFINITIONS

SECTION 201
GENERAL

201.1 Scope. Unless otherwise expressly stated, the following terms shall, for the purposes of this code, have the meanings shown in this chapter.

201.2 Interchangeability. Words stated in the present tense include the future; words stated in the masculine gender include the feminine and neuter; the singular number includes the plural and the plural, the singular.

201.3 Terms defined in other codes. Where terms are not defined in this code and are defined in the *Building Code of New York State, Fire Code of New York State, Plumbing Code of New York State, Mechanical Code of New York State, Fuel Gas Code of New York State,* the *Residential Code of New York State,* the *Energy Conservation Construction Code of New York State* or the *Existing Building Code of New York State,* such terms shall have the meanings ascribed to them as in those codes.

201.4 Terms not defined. Where terms are not defined through the methods authorized by this section, such terms shall have ordinarily accepted meanings such as the context implies.

201.5 Parts. Whenever the words "dwelling unit," "dwelling," "premises," "building," "rooming house," "rooming unit," "housekeeping unit" or "story" are stated in this code, they shall be construed as though they were followed by the words "or any part thereof."

SECTION 202
GENERAL DEFINITIONS

APPROVED. Approved by the code enforcement official.

AUTHORITY HAVING JURISDICTION. The local government, county government or state agency responsible for the administration and enforcement of an applicable regulation or law.

BASEMENT. That portion of a building which is partly or completely below grade.

BATHROOM. A room containing plumbing fixtures including a bathtub or shower.

BEDROOM. Any room or space used or intended to be used for sleeping purposes in either a dwelling or sleeping unit.

CODE ENFORCEMENT OFFICIAL. The officer or other designated authority charged with the administration and enforcement of this code, or a duly authorized representative.

CONDEMN. To adjudge unfit for occupancy.

[B] DWELLING UNIT. A single unit providing complete, independent living facilities for one or more persons, including permanent provisions for living, sleeping, eating, cooking and sanitation.

EASEMENT. That portion of land or property reserved for present or future use by a person or agency other than the legal fee owner(s) of the property. The easement shall be permitted to be for use under, on or above a said lot or lots.

EXTERIOR PROPERTY. The open space on the premises and on adjoining property under the control of owners or operators of such premises.

EXTERMINATION. The control and elimination of insects, rats or other pests by eliminating their harborage places; by removing or making inaccessible materials that serve as their food; by poison spraying, fumigating, trapping or by any other approved pest elimination methods.

GARBAGE. The animal or vegetable waste resulting from the handling, preparation, cooking and consumption of food.

GUARD. A building component or a system of building components located at or near the open sides of elevated walking surfaces that minimizes the possibility of a fall from the walking surface to a lower level.

HABITABLE SPACE. Space in a structure for living, sleeping, eating or cooking. Bathrooms, toilet rooms, closets, halls, storage or utility spaces, and similar areas are not considered habitable spaces.

HOUSEKEEPING UNIT. A room or group of rooms forming a single habitable space equipped and intended to be used for living, sleeping, cooking and eating which does not contain, within such a unit, a toilet, lavatory and bathtub or shower.

IMMINENT DANGER. A condition which could cause serious or life-threatening injury or death at any time.

INFESTATION. The presence, within or contiguous to, a structure or premises of insects, rats, vermin or other pests.

INOPERABLE MOTOR VEHICLE. A motor vehicle which cannot be driven upon the public streets for reasons including but not limited to being unlicensed, wrecked, abandoned, in a state of disrepair, or incapable of being moved under its own power.

LABELED. Devices, equipment, appliances, or materials to which has been affixed a label, seal, symbol or other identifying mark of a nationally recognized testing laboratory, inspection agency or other organization concerned with product evaluation that maintains periodic inspection of the production of the above-labeled items and by whose label the manufacturer attests to compliance with applicable nationally recognized standards.

LET FOR OCCUPANCY OR LET. To permit, provide or offer possession or occupancy of a dwelling, dwelling unit, rooming unit, building, premise or structure by a person who is or is not the legal owner of record thereof, pursuant to a written or unwritten lease, agreement or license, or pursuant

DEFINITIONS

to a recorded or unrecorded agreement of contract for the sale of land.

OCCUPANCY. The purpose for which a building or portion thereof is utilized or occupied.

OCCUPANT. Any individual living or sleeping in a building, or having possession of a space within a building.

OPENABLE AREA. That part of a window, skylight or door which is available for unobstructed ventilation and which opens directly to the outdoors.

OPERATOR. Any person who has charge, care or control of a structure or premises which is let or offered for occupancy.

OWNER. Any person, agent, operator, firm or corporation having a legal or equitable interest in the property; or recorded in the official records of the state, county or municipality as holding title to the property; or otherwise having control of the property, including the guardian of the estate of any such person, and the executor or administrator of the estate of such person if ordered to take possession of real property by a court.

PERSON. An individual, corporation, partnership or any other group acting as a unit.

PREMISES. A lot, plot or parcel of land, easement or public way, including any structures thereon.

PUBLIC WAY. Any street, alley or similar parcel of land essentially unobstructed from the ground to the sky, which is deeded, dedicated or otherwise permanently appropriated to the public for public use.

ROOMING HOUSE. A building arranged or occupied for lodging, with or without meals, for compensation and not occupied as a one- or two-family dwelling.

ROOMING UNIT. Any room or group of rooms forming a single habitable unit occupied or intended to be occupied for sleeping or living, but not for cooking purposes.

RUBBISH. Combustible and noncombustible waste materials, except garbage; the term shall include the residue from the burning of wood, coal, coke and other combustible materials, paper, rags, cartons, boxes, wood, excelsior, rubber, leather, tree branches, yard trimmings, tin cans, metals, mineral matter, glass, crockery and dust and other similar materials; this term shall also include discarded, abandoned or stored refrigerators.

[B] SLEEPING UNIT. A room or space in which people sleep, which can also include permanent provisions for living, eating and either sanitation or kitchen facilities, but not both. Such rooms and spaces that are also part of a dwelling unit are not sleeping units.

STRUCTURE. That which is built or constructed or a portion thereof.

SWIMMING POOL. Any structure, basin, chamber or tank which is intended for swimming, diving, recreational bathing or wading and which contains, is designed to contain, or is capable of containing water more than 24 inches (610 mm) deep at any point. This includes in-ground, above-ground and on-ground pools; indoor pools; hot tubs; spas; and fixed-in-place wading pools.

TENANT. A person, corporation, partnership or group, whether or not the legal owner of record, occupying a building or portion thereof as a unit.

TOILET ROOM. A room containing a water closet or urinal but not a bathtub or shower.

VENTILATION. The natural or mechanical process of supplying conditioned or unconditioned air to, or removing such air from, any space.

WORKMANLIKE. Executed in a skilled manner; e.g., generally plumb, level, square, in line, undamaged and without marring adjacent work.

YARD. An open space on the same lot with a structure.

CHAPTER 3
GENERAL REQUIREMENTS

SECTION 301
GENERAL

301.1 Scope. The provisions of this chapter shall govern the minimum conditions and the responsibilities of persons for maintenance of structures, equipment and exterior property.

301.2 Responsibility. The owner of the premises shall maintain the structures and exterior property in compliance with these requirements, except as otherwise provided for in this code. A person shall not occupy as owner-occupant or permit another person to occupy premises which are not in a sanitary and safe condition and which do not comply with the requirements of this chapter. Occupants of a dwelling unit, rooming unit or housekeeping unit are responsible for keeping in a clean, sanitary and safe condition that part of the dwelling unit, rooming unit, housekeeping unit or premises which they occupy and control.

301.3 Vacant structures and land. All vacant structures and premises thereof or vacant land shall be maintained in a clean, safe, secure and sanitary condition as provided herein so as not to cause a blighting problem or adversely affect the public health or safety.

SECTION 302
EXTERIOR PROPERTY AREAS

302.1 Sanitation. All exterior property and premises shall be maintained in a clean, safe and sanitary condition. The occupant shall keep that part of the exterior property which such occupant occupies or controls in a clean and sanitary condition.

302.2 Grading and drainage. All premises shall be graded and maintained to prevent the erosion of soil and to prevent the accumulation of stagnant water thereon, or within any structure located thereon.

Exception: Approved retention areas and reservoirs.

302.3 Sidewalks and driveways. All sidewalks, walkways, stairs, driveways, parking spaces and similar areas shall be kept in a proper state of repair, and maintained free from hazardous conditions.

302.3.1 Off street parking lots. Whenever a person, firm or corporation performs the following work in an off street parking lot, within a six month period of time, the design of designated accessible parking shall be in accordance with the requirements of the *Building Code of New York State* Section 1106 and the design features found in this section.

1. Repave or repaint more than one half of the total number of parking spaces in an off street parking lot, which contains designated accessible parking spaces.

2. Creates designated accessible parking spaces in an off street parking lot.

3. Repave or repaint more than one half of the total number of designated accessible parking spaces in an off street parking lot.

Designated accessible parking spaces shall incorporate the following design features:

Spaces

The parking space shall be 96 inches (2438 mm) wide minimum and shall have an adjacent access aisle of 96 inches (2438 mm) wide minimum.

Two parking spaces shall be permitted to share a common access aisle.

Access aisle shall extend the full length of the parking space they serve and shall have a surface slope not steeper than 1:48.

Signage

Each accessible parking space shall be provided with signage displaying the international symbol of accessibility.

Each access aisle shall be provided with signage reading, "No Parking Anytime." Signs shall be permanently installed at a clear height of between 60 inches (1525 mm) and 84 inches (2185 mm) above grade and shall not interfere with an accessible route from an access aisle.

302.4 Weeds. All premises and immediate exterior property shall be maintained free from weeds or plant growth in excess of 10 inches (254 mm). All noxious weeds shall be prohibited. Weeds shall be defined as all grasses, annual plants and vegetation, other than trees or shrubs provided; however, this term shall not include cultivated flowers and gardens.

302.5 Rodent harborage. All structures and exterior property shall be kept free from rodent harborage and infestation. Where rodents are found, they shall be promptly exterminated by approved processes which will not be injurious to human health. After extermination, proper precautions shall be taken to eliminate rodent harborage and prevent reinfestation.

302.6 Exhaust vents. Pipes, ducts, conductors, fans or blowers shall not discharge gases, steam, vapor, hot air, grease, smoke, odors or other gaseous or particulate wastes directly upon abutting or adjacent public or private property or that of another tenant.

302.7 Accessory structures. All accessory structures, including detached garages, fences and walls, shall be maintained structurally sound and in good repair.

302.8 Motor vehicles. Except as otherwise provided for in statute or other regulations, two or more inoperative or unlicensed motor vehicles shall not be parked, kept or stored on any premises, and no vehicle shall at any time be in a state of major disassembly, disrepair, or in the process of being stripped or dismantled. Painting of vehicles is prohibited unless conducted inside an approved spray booth.

> **Exception:** A vehicle of any type is permitted to undergo major overhaul, including body work, provided that such work is performed inside a structure or similarly enclosed area designed and approved for such purposes.

SECTION 303
SWIMMING POOLS, SPAS AND HOT TUBS

303.1 Swimming pools. Swimming pools shall be maintained in a clean and sanitary condition, and in good repair.

[B] 303.2 Enclosures. The provisions of this section shall control the design of barriers for residential swimming pools, spas and hot tubs. For public swimming pools, spas and hot tubs refer to Chapter 31 of the *Building Code of New York State*. Design controls are intended to provide protection against potential drownings and near-drownings by restricting access to swimming pools, spas and hot tubs.

> **Exception:** Spas or hot tubs with a safety cover that complies with ASTM F 1346 shall be exempt from the provisions of this section.

303.3 Outdoor swimming pool. An outdoor swimming pool, including an in-ground, aboveground or on-ground pool, hot tub or spa shall be provided with a barrier which shall comply with the following:

1. The top of the barrier shall be at least 48 inches (1219 mm) above grade measured on the side of the barrier which faces away from the swimming pool. The maximum vertical clearance between grade and the bottom of the barrier shall be 2 inches (51 mm) measured on the side of the barrier which faces away from the swimming pool. Where the top of the pool structure is above grade, such as an aboveground pool, the barrier may be at ground level, such as the pool structure, or mounted on top of the pool structure. Where the barrier is mounted on top of the pool structure, the maximum vertical clearance between the top of the pool structure and the bottom of the barrier shall be 4 inches (102 mm).

2. Openings in the barrier shall not allow passage of a 4-inch-diameter (102 mm) sphere.

3. Solid barriers which do not have openings, such as a masonry or stone wall, shall not contain indentations or protrusions except for normal construction tolerances and tooled masonry joints.

4. Where the barrier is composed of horizontal and vertical members and the distance between the tops of the horizontal members is less than 45 inches (1143 mm), the horizontal members shall be located on the swimming pool side of the fence. Spacing between vertical members shall not exceed 1.75 inches (44 mm) in width. Where there are decorative cutouts within vertical members, spacing within the cutouts shall not exceed 1.75 inches (44 mm) in width.

5. Where the barrier is composed of horizontal and vertical members and the distance between the tops of the horizontal members is 45 inches (1143 mm) or more, spacing between vertical members shall not exceed 4 inches (102 mm). Where there are decorative cutouts within vertical members, spacing within the cutouts shall not exceed 1.75 inches (44 mm) in width

6. Maximum mesh size for chain link fences shall be a 2.25-inch (32 mm) square unless the fence is provided with slats fastened at the top or the bottom which reduce the openings to not more than 1.75 inches (44 mm).

7. Where the barrier is composed of diagonal members, such as a lattice fence, the maximum opening formed by the diagonal members shall not be more than 1.75 inches (44 mm).

8. Access gates shall comply with the requirements of Section 303.3, Items 1 through 7, and shall be securely locked with a key, combination or other child-proof lock sufficient to prevent access to the swimming pool through such gate when the swimming pool is not in use or supervised. Pedestrian access gates shall open outward away from the pool and shall be self-closing and have a self-latching device. Gates other than pedestrian access gates shall have a self-latching device. Where the release mechanism of the self-latching device is located less than 54 inches (1372 mm) from the bottom of the gate, the release mechanism and openings shall comply with the following:

    8.1. The release mechanism shall be located on the pool side of the gate at least 3 inches (76 mm) below the top of the gate, and

    8.2. The gate and barrier shall have no opening greater than 0.5 inch (12.7 mm) within 18 inches (457 mm) of the release mechanism.

9. Where a wall of a dwelling serves as part of the barrier one of the following conditions shall be met:

    9.1. The pool shall be equipped with a powered safety cover in compliance with ASTM F 1346; or

    9.2. All doors with direct access to the pool through that wall shall be equipped with an alarm which produces an audible warning when the door and/or its screen, if present, are opened. The alarm shall be listed in accordance with UL 2017. The audible alarm shall activate within 7 seconds and sound continuously for a minimum of 30 seconds immediately after the door and/or its screen, if present, are opened and be capable of being heard throughout the house during normal household activities. The alarm shall automatically reset under all conditions. The alarm system shall be equipped with a manual means, such as touch pad or switch, to temporarily deactivate the alarm for a single opening. Deactivation shall last for not more than 15 seconds. The deactivation switch(es) shall be located at least 54 inches (1372 mm) above the threshold of the door; or

9.3. Other means of protection, such as self-closing doors with self-latching devices shall be acceptable so long as the degree of protection afforded is not less than the protection afforded by Item 9.1 or 9.2 described above.

10. Where an aboveground pool structure is used as a barrier or where the barrier is mounted on top of the pool structure, and the means of access is a ladder or steps, then:

10.1. The ladder or steps shall be capable of being secured, locked or removed to prevent access, or

10.2. The ladder or steps shall be surrounded by a barrier which meets the requirements of Section 303.3, Items 1 through 9. When the ladder or steps are secured, locked or removed, any opening created shall not allow the passage of a 4-inch-diameter (102 mm) sphere.

303.4 Indoor swimming pool. All walls surrounding an indoor swimming pool shall comply with Section 303.3, Item 9.

303.5 Prohibited locations. Barriers shall be located so as to prohibit permanent structures, equipment or similar objects from being used to climb the barriers.

303.6 Swimming pool and spa alarms. Spas or hot tubs with a safety cover which complies with ASTM F 1346, shall be exempt from the provisions of this section.

303.6.1 Applicability. A swimming pool or spa installed, constructed or substantially modified after December 14, 2006, shall be equipped with an approved pool alarm.

Exceptions:

1. A hot tub or spa equipped with a safety cover which complies with ASTM F 1346.

2. A swimming pool (other than a hot tub or spa) equipped with an automatic power safety cover which complies with ASTM F 1346.

Pool alarms shall comply with ASTM F 2208 and shall be installed, used and maintained in accordance with the manufacturer's instructions and this section.

303.6.2 Multiple alarms. A pool alarm must be capable of detecting entry into the water at any point on the surface of the swimming pool. If necessary to provide detection capability at every point on the surface of the swimming pool, more than one pool alarm shall be provided.

303.6.3 Alarm activation. Pool alarms shall activate upon detecting entry into the water and shall sound poolside and inside the dwelling.

303.6.4 Prohibited alarms. The use of personal immersion alarms shall not be construed as compliance with this section.

303.7 Temporary barriers. An outdoor swimming pool, including an in-ground, above-ground or on-ground pool, hot tub or spa shall be surrounded by a temporary barrier during installation or construction and shall remain in place until a permanent barrier in compliance with Section 303.3 is provided.

Exceptions:

1. Above-ground or on-ground pools where the pool structure is the barrier in compliance with Section 303.3.

2. Spas or hot tubs with a safety cover which complies with ASTM F 1346, provided that such safety cover is in place during the period of installation or construction of such hot tub or spa. The temporary removal of a safety cover as required to facilitate the installation or construction of a hot tub or spa during periods when at least one person engaged in the installation or construction is present is permitted.

303.7.1 Height. The top of the temporary barrier shall be at least 48 inches (1219 mm) above grade measured on the side of the barrier which faces away from the swimming pool.

303.7.2 Replacement by a permanent barrier. A temporary barrier shall be replaced by a complying permanent barrier within either of the following periods:

1. 90 days of the date of issuance of the building permit for the installation or construction of the swimming pool; or

2. 90 days of the date of commencement of the installation or construction of the swimming pool.

303.7.2.1 Replacement extension. Subject to the approval of the code enforcement official, the time period for completion of the permanent barrier may be extended for good cause, including, but not limited to, adverse weather conditions delaying construction.

303.8 Entrapment protection for swimming pools and spas. Swimming pools and spas shall maintain body entrapment protections for suction outlets in accordance with the *Building Code of New York State* or the *Residential Code of New York State*, as applicable.

SECTION 304
EXTERIOR STRUCTURE

304.1 General. The exterior of a structure shall be maintained in good repair, structurally sound and sanitary so as not to pose a threat to the public health, safety or welfare.

304.2 Protective treatment. All exterior surfaces, including but not limited to, doors, door and window frames, cornices, porches, trim, balconies, decks and fences shall be maintained in good condition. Exterior wood surfaces, other than decay-resistant woods, shall be protected from the elements and decay by painting or other protective covering or treatment. Peeling, flaking and chipped paint shall be eliminated and surfaces repainted. In addition to requirements of this code, 40 CFR 745 (titled "Lead-based Paint Poisoning Prevention in Certain Residential Structures"), a regulation

GENERAL REQUIREMENTS

issued and enforced by the Federal Environmental Protection Agency, applies to certain activities in buildings that may contain lead-based paint, including renovations performed for compensation in "target housing" and "child-occupied facilities," "abatement" of lead-based paint hazards and other "lead-based paint activities" (as those terms are defined in 40 CFR Part 745). All siding and masonry joints as well as those between the building envelope and the perimeter of windows, doors, and skylights shall be maintained weather resistant and water tight. All metal surfaces subject to rust or corrosion shall be coated to inhibit such rust and corrosion and all surfaces with rust or corrosion shall be stabilized and coated to inhibit future rust and corrosion. Oxidation stains shall be removed from exterior surfaces. Surfaces designed for stabilization by oxidation are exempt from this requirement.

[F] 304.3 Premises identification. Buildings shall have approved address numbers placed in a position to be plainly legible and visible from the street or road fronting the property. These numbers shall contrast with their background. Address numbers shall be Arabic numerals or alphabet letters. Numbers shall be a minimum of 4 inches (102 mm) high with a minimum stroke width of 0.5 inch (12.7 mm).

> **Exception:** Buildings identified under an addressing scheme as part of a countywide 911 numbering system.

304.4 Structural members. All structural members shall be maintained free from deterioration, and shall be capable of safely supporting the imposed dead and live loads.

304.5 Foundation walls. All foundation walls shall be maintained plumb and free from open cracks and breaks and shall be kept in such condition so as to prevent the entry of rodents and other pests.

304.6 Exterior walls. All exterior walls shall be free from holes, breaks, and loose or rotting materials; and maintained weatherproof and properly surface coated where required to prevent deterioration.

304.7 Roofs and drainage. The roof and flashing shall be sound, tight and not have defects that admit rain. Roof drainage shall be adequate to prevent dampness or deterioration in the walls or interior portion of the structure. Roof drains, gutters and downspouts shall be maintained in good repair and free from obstructions. Roof water shall not be discharged in a manner that creates a public nuisance.

304.8 Decorative features. All cornices, belt courses, corbels, terra cotta trim, wall facings and similar decorative features shall be maintained in good repair with proper anchorage and in a safe condition.

304.9 Overhang extensions. All overhang extensions including, but not limited to canopies, marquees, signs, metal awnings, fire escapes, standpipes and exhaust ducts shall be maintained in good repair and be properly anchored so as to be kept in a sound condition. When required, all exposed surfaces of metal or wood shall be protected from the elements and against decay or rust by periodic application of weather-coating materials, such as paint or similar surface treatment.

304.10 Stairways, decks, porches and balconies. Every exterior stairway, deck, porch and balcony, and all appurtenances attached thereto, shall be maintained structurally sound, in good repair, with proper anchorage and capable of supporting the imposed loads.

304.11 Chimneys and towers. All chimneys, cooling towers, smoke stacks, and similar appurtenances shall be maintained structurally safe and sound, and in good repair. All exposed surfaces of metal or wood shall be protected from the elements and against decay or rust by periodic application of weather-coating materials, such as paint or similar surface treatment.

304.12 Handrails and guards. Every handrail and guard shall be firmly fastened and capable of supporting normally imposed loads and shall be maintained in good condition.

304.13 Window, skylight and door frames. Every window, skylight, door and frame shall be kept in sound condition, good repair and weather tight.

> **304.13.1 Glazing.** All glazing materials shall be maintained free from cracks and holes.

> **304.13.2 Openable windows.** Every window, other than a fixed window, shall be easily openable and capable of being held in position by window hardware.

304.14 Reserved.

304.15 Doors. All exterior doors, door assemblies and hardware shall be maintained in good condition. Locks at all entrances to dwelling units and sleeping units shall tightly secure the door. Locks on means of egress doors shall be in accordance with Section 703.3.

304.16 Basement hatchways. Every basement hatchway shall be maintained to prevent the entrance of rodents, rain and surface drainage water.

304.17 Guards for basement windows. Every basement window that is openable shall be supplied with rodent shields, storm windows or other approved protection against the entry of rodents.

304.18 Reserved.

SECTION 305
INTERIOR STRUCTURE

305.1 General. The interior of a structure and equipment therein shall be maintained in good repair, structurally sound and in a sanitary condition. Occupants shall keep that part of the structure which they occupy or control in a clean and sanitary condition. Every owner of a structure containing a rooming house, housekeeping units, a hotel, a dormitory, two or more dwelling units or two or more nonresidential occupancies, shall maintain, in a clean and sanitary condition, the shared or public areas of the structure and exterior property.

305.2 Structural members. All structural members shall be maintained structurally sound, and be capable of supporting the imposed loads.

305.3 Interior surfaces. All interior surfaces, including windows and doors, shall be maintained in good, clean and sanitary condition. Peeling, chipping, flaking or abraded paint shall be repaired, removed or covered. In addition to requirements of this code, 40 CFR 745 (titled "Lead-based Paint Poisoning Prevention in Certain Residential Structures"), a regulation issued and enforced by the Federal Environmental Protection Agency, applies to certain activities in buildings that may contain lead-based paint, including renovations performed for compensation in "target housing" and "child-occupied facilities," "abatement" of lead-based paint hazards and other "lead-based paint activities" (as those terms are defined in 40 CFR Part 745). Cracked or loose plaster, decayed wood and other defective surface conditions shall be corrected.

305.4 Stairs and walking surfaces. Every stair, ramp, landing, balcony, porch, deck or other walking surface shall be maintained in sound condition and good repair.

305.5 Handrails and guards. Every handrail and guard shall be firmly fastened and capable of supporting normally imposed loads and shall be maintained in good condition.

305.6 Interior doors. Every interior door shall fit reasonably well within its frame and shall be capable of being opened and closed by being properly and securely attached to jambs, headers or tracks as intended by the manufacturer of the attachment hardware.

SECTION 306
HANDRAILS AND GUARDRAILS

306.1 General. Every exterior and interior flight of stairs having more than four risers shall have a handrail on one side of the stair, and every open portion of a stair, landing, balcony, porch, deck, ramp or other walking surface which is more than 30 inches (762 mm) above the floor or grade below shall have guards. Handrails shall not be less than 30 inches (762 mm) high or more than 42 inches (1067 mm) high measured vertically above the nosing of the tread or above the finished floor of the landing or walking surfaces. Guards shall not be less than 30 inches (762 mm) high above the floor of the landing, balcony, porch, deck, or ramp or other walking surface.

Exception: Guards shall not be required where exempted by the *Building Code of New York State*.

SECTION 307
RUBBISH AND GARBAGE

307.1 Accumulation of rubbish or garbage. All exterior property and premises, and the interior of every structure, shall be free from any accumulation of rubbish or garbage.

307.1.1 Dry vegetation, combustible waste and refuse. Combustible waste, refuse and large quantities of dry vegetation which by reason of their proximity to buildings or structures would constitute a fire hazard or contribute to the spread of fire shall be removed.

307.2 Disposal of rubbish. Every occupant of a structure shall dispose of all rubbish in a clean and sanitary manner by placing such rubbish in approved containers.

307.2.1 Rubbish storage facilities. The owner of every occupied premises shall supply approved covered containers for rubbish, and the owner of the premises shall be responsible for the removal of rubbish.

307.2.2 Refrigerators. Refrigerators and similar equipment shall not be discarded, abandoned or stored on premises accessible to children without first removing the doors.

307.3 Disposal of garbage. Every occupant of a structure shall dispose of garbage in a clean and sanitary manner by placing such garbage in an approved garbage disposal facility or approved garbage containers.

307.3.1 Garbage facilities. The owner of every dwelling shall supply one of the following: an approved mechanical food waste grinder in each dwelling unit; an approved incinerator unit in the structure available to the occupants in each dwelling unit; or an approved leakproof, covered, outside garbage container.

307.3.2 Containers. The operator of every establishment producing garbage shall provide, and at all times cause to be utilized, approved leakproof containers provided with close-fitting covers for the storage of such materials until removed from the premises for disposal.

SECTION 308
EXTERMINATION

308.1 Infestation. All structures shall be kept free from insect and rodent infestation. All structures in which insects or rodents are found shall be promptly exterminated by approved processes that will not be injurious to human health. After extermination, proper precautions shall be taken to prevent reinfestation.

308.2 Owner. The owner of any structure shall be responsible for extermination within the structure prior to renting or leasing the structure.

308.3 Single occupant. The occupant of a one-family dwelling or of a single-tenant nonresidential structure shall be responsible for extermination on the premises.

308.4 Multiple occupancy. The owner of a structure containing two or more dwelling units, a multiple occupancy, a rooming house or a nonresidential structure shall be responsible for extermination in the public or shared areas of the structure and exterior property. If infestation is caused by failure of an occupant to prevent such infestation in the area occupied, the occupant shall be responsible for extermination.

308.5 Occupant. The occupant of any structure shall be responsible for the continued rodent and pest-free condition of the structure.

Exception: Where the infestations are caused by defects in the structure, the owner shall be responsible for extermination.

CHAPTER 4
LIGHT, VENTILATION AND OCCUPANCY LIMITATIONS

SECTION 401
GENERAL

401.1 Scope. The provisions of this chapter shall govern the minimum conditions and standards for light, ventilation and space for occupying a structure.

401.2 Responsibility. The owner of the structure shall provide and maintain light, ventilation and space conditions in compliance with these requirements. A person shall not occupy as owner-occupant, or permit another person to occupy, any premises that do not comply with the requirements of this chapter.

401.3 Alternative devices. In lieu of the means for natural light and ventilation herein prescribed, artificial light or mechanical ventilation complying with the *Residential Code of New York State* or the *Building Code of New York State* shall be permitted.

SECTION 402
LIGHT

402.1 Habitable spaces. Every habitable space shall have at least one window of approved size facing directly to the outdoors or to a court. The minimum total glazed area for every habitable space shall be 8 percent of the floor area of such room. Wherever walls or other portions of a structure face a window of any room and such obstructions are located less than 3 feet (914 mm) from the window and extend to a level above that of the ceiling of the room, such window shall not be deemed to face directly to the outdoors nor to a court and shall not be included as contributing to the required minimum total window area for the room.

> **Exception:** Where natural light for rooms or spaces without exterior glazing areas is provided through an adjoining room, the unobstructed opening to the adjoining room shall be at least 8 percent of the floor area of the interior room or space, but not less than 25 square feet (2.33 m^2). The exterior glazing area shall be based on the total floor area being served.

402.2 Common halls and stairways. Every common hall and stairway in residential occupancies, other than in one- and two-family dwellings, shall be lighted at all times with at least a 60-watt standard incandescent light bulb for each 200 square feet (19 m^2) of floor area or equivalent illumination, provided that the spacing between lights shall not be greater than 30 feet (9144 mm). In other than residential occupancies, means of egress, including exterior means of egress, stairways shall be illuminated at all times the building space served by the means of egress is occupied with a minimum of 1 footcandle (11 lux) at floors, landings and treads.

402.3 Other spaces. All other spaces shall be provided with natural or artificial light sufficient to permit the maintenance of sanitary conditions, and the safe occupancy of the space and utilization of the appliances, equipment and fixtures.

SECTION 403
VENTILATION

403.1 Habitable spaces. Every habitable space shall have at least one openable window. The total openable area of the window in every room shall be equal to at least 45 percent of the minimum glazed area required in Section 402.1.

> **Exception:** Where rooms and spaces without openings to the outdoors are ventilated through an adjoining room, the unobstructed opening to the adjoining room shall be at least 8 percent of the floor area of the interior room or space, but not less than 25 square feet (2.33 m^2). The ventilation openings to the outdoors shall be based on a total floor area being ventilated.

403.2 Bathrooms and toilet rooms. Every bathroom and toilet room shall comply with the ventilation requirements for habitable spaces as required by Section 403.1, except that a window shall not be required in such spaces equipped with a mechanical ventilation system. Air exhausted by a mechanical ventilation system from a bathroom or toilet room shall discharge to the outdoors and shall not be recirculated.

403.3 Cooking facilities. Cooking shall not be permitted in any rooming unit or dormitory unit, and a cooking facility or appliance shall not be permitted to be present in a rooming unit or dormitory unit.

> **Exception:** Devices such as coffeepots and microwave ovens shall not be considered cooking appliances.

403.4 Process ventilation. Where injurious, toxic, irritating or noxious fumes, gases, dusts or mists are generated, a local exhaust ventilation system shall be provided to remove the contaminating agent at the source. Contaminated air shall be exhausted to the exterior and not be recirculated to any space.

403.5 Clothes dryer exhaust. Clothes dryer exhaust systems shall be independent of all other systems and shall be exhausted in accordance with the manufacturer's instructions.

SECTION 404
OCCUPANCY LIMITATIONS

404.1 Privacy. Dwelling units, hotel units, housekeeping units, rooming units and dormitory units shall be arranged to provide privacy and be separate from other adjoining spaces.

404.2 Minimum room widths. A habitable room, other than a kitchen, shall not be less than 7 feet (2134 mm) in any plan dimension. Kitchens shall have a clear passageway of not less than 3 feet (914 mm) between counterfronts and appliances or counterfronts and walls.

Exceptions:

1. Manufactured housing regulated in the *Residential Code of New York State* shall be permitted to retain room dimensions provided for at time of manufacture.

2. Spaces legally in existence before January 1, 2003, and spaces for which a variance has been legally granted shall be allowed to be occupied.

404.3 Minimum ceiling heights. Habitable spaces, hallways, corridors, laundry areas, bathrooms, toilet rooms and habitable basement areas shall have a clear ceiling height of not less than 7 feet (2134 mm).

Exceptions:

1. In one- and two-family dwellings, beams or girders spaced not less than 4 feet (1219 mm) on center and projecting not more than 6 inches (152 mm) below the required ceiling height.

2. Basement rooms in one- and two-family dwellings occupied exclusively for laundry, study or recreation purposes, having a ceiling height of not less than 6 feet, 8 inches (2033 mm) with not less than 6 feet, 4 inches (1932 mm) of clear height under beams, girders, ducts and similar obstructions.

3. Rooms occupied exclusively for sleeping, study or similar purposes and having a sloped ceiling over all or part of the room, with a clear ceiling height of at least 7 feet (2134 mm) over not less than one-third of the required minimum floor area. In calculating the floor area of such rooms, only those portions of the floor area with a clear ceiling height of 5 feet (1524 mm) or more shall be included.

4. Manufactured housing regulated in the *Residential Code of New York State* shall be permitted to retain ceiling heights provided at time of manufacture.

5. Spaces legally in existence before January 1, 2003, and spaces for which a variance has been legally granted shall be allowed to be occupied.

6. Ceiling heights reduced by necessary repairs shall be no lower than 6 feet, 8 inches.

404.4 Bedroom requirements. Every bedroom shall comply with the requirements of Sections 404.4.1 through 404.4.5.

404.4.1 Area for sleeping purposes. Every bedroom occupied by one person shall contain at least 70 square feet (6.5 m^2) of floor area, and every bedroom occupied by more than one person shall contain at least 50 square feet (4.6 m^2) of floor area for each occupant thereof.

404.4.2 Access from bedrooms. Bedrooms shall not constitute the only means of access to other bedrooms or habitable spaces and shall not serve as the only means of egress from other habitable spaces.

Exception: Units that contain fewer than two bedrooms.

404.4.3 Water closet accessibility. Every bedroom shall have access to at least one water closet and one lavatory without passing through another bedroom. Every bedroom in a dwelling unit shall have access to at least one water closet and lavatory located in the same story as the bedroom or an adjacent story.

Exception: Owner-occupied, one-family dwellings.

404.4.4 Prohibited occupancy. Kitchens and nonhabitable spaces shall not be used for sleeping purposes.

404.4.5 Other requirements. Bedrooms shall comply with the applicable provisions of this code including, but not limited to, the light, ventilation, room area, ceiling height and room width requirements of this chapter; the plumbing facilities and water-heating facilities requirements of Chapter 5; the heating facilities and electrical receptacle requirements of Chapter 6; and the smoke detector and emergency escape requirements of Chapter 7.

404.5 Overcrowding. Dwelling units shall not be occupied by more occupants than permitted by the minimum area requirements of Table 404.5.

**TABLE 404.5
MINIMUM AREA REQUIREMENTS**

SPACE	MINIMUM AREA IN SQUARE FEET		
	1-2 occupants	3-5 occupants	6 or more occupants
Living room[a,b]	No requirements	120	150
Dining room[a,b]	No requirements	80	100
Kitchen	50	50	60
Bedrooms	Shall comply with Section 404.4		

For SI: 1 square foot = 0.0929 m^2.

a. See Section 404.5.2 for combined living room/dining room spaces.
b. See Section 404.5.1 for limitations on determining the minimum occupancy area for sleeping purposes.

404.5.1 Sleeping area. The minimum occupancy area required by Table 404.5 shall not be included as a sleeping area in determining the minimum occupancy area for sleeping purposes. All sleeping areas shall comply with Section 404.4.

404.5.2 Combined spaces. Combined living room and dining room spaces shall comply with the requirements of Table 404.5 if the total area is equal to that required for separate rooms and if the space is located so as to function as a combination living room/dining room.

404.6 Efficiency unit. Nothing in this section shall prohibit an efficiency living unit from meeting the following requirements:

1. A unit occupied by not more than two occupants shall have a clear floor area of not less than 220 square feet (20.4 m^2). A unit occupied by three occupants shall have a clear floor area of not less than 320 square feet (29.7 m^2). These required areas shall be exclusive of the areas required by Items 2 and 3.

2. The unit shall be provided with a kitchen sink, cooking appliance and refrigeration facilities, each having a clear working space of not less than 30 inches (762 mm) in front. Light and ventilation conforming to this code shall be provided.

Don't Miss Out On Valuable ICC Membership Benefits. Join ICC Today!

Join the largest and most respected building code and safety organization. As an official member of the International Code Council®, these great ICC® benefits are at your fingertips.

EXCLUSIVE MEMBER DISCOUNTS
ICC members enjoy exclusive discounts on codes, technical publications, seminars, plan reviews, educational materials, videos, and other products and services.

TECHNICAL SUPPORT
ICC members get expert code support services, opinions, and technical assistance from experienced engineers and architects, backed by the world's leading repository of code publications.

FREE CODE—LATEST EDITION
Most new individual members receive a free code from the latest edition of the International Codes®. New corporate and governmental members receive one set of major International Codes (Building, Residential, Fire, Fuel Gas, Mechanical, Plumbing, Private Sewage Disposal).

FREE CODE MONOGRAPHS
Code monographs and other materials on proposed International Code revisions are provided free to ICC members upon request.

PROFESSIONAL DEVELOPMENT
Receive Member Discounts for on-site training, institutes, symposiums, audio virtual seminars, and on-line training! ICC delivers educational programs that enable members to transition to the I-Codes®, interpret and enforce codes, perform plan reviews, design and build safe structures, and perform administrative functions more effectively and with greater efficiency. Members also enjoy special educational offerings that provide a forum to learn about and discuss current and emerging issues that affect the building industry.

ENHANCE YOUR CAREER
ICC keeps you current on the latest building codes, methods, and materials. Our conferences, job postings, and educational programs can also help you advance your career.

CODE NEWS
ICC members have the inside track for code news and industry updates via e-mails, newsletters, conferences, chapter meetings, networking, and the ICC website (www.iccsafe.org). Obtain code opinions, reports, adoption updates, and more. Without exception, ICC is your number one source for the very latest code and safety standards information.

MEMBER RECOGNITION
Improve your standing and prestige among your peers. ICC member cards, wall certificates, and logo decals identify your commitment to the community and to the safety of people worldwide.

ICC NETWORKING
Take advantage of exciting new opportunities to network with colleagues, future employers, potential business partners, industry experts, and more than 50,000 ICC members. ICC also has over 300 chapters across North America and around the globe to help you stay informed on local events, to consult with other professionals, and to enhance your reputation in the local community.

JOIN NOW! 1-888-422-7233, x33804 | www.iccsafe.org/membership

INTERNATIONAL CODE COUNCIL®

People Helping People Build a Safer World™

This insert is not part of the official text of the New York State Uniform Fire Prevention and Building Code or New York State Energy Conservation Code.

VALUABLE GUIDES TO THE 2006 I-CODES®

FULL COLOR! HUNDREDS OF PHOTOS AND ILLUSTRATIONS!

 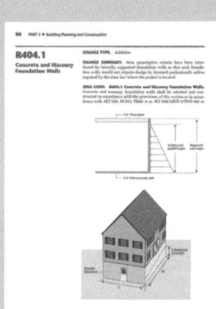 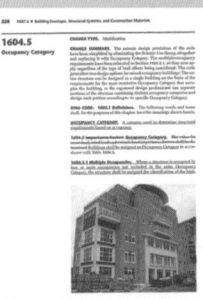 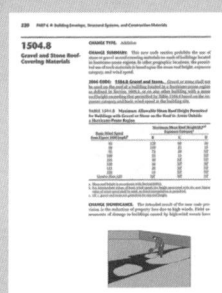

SIGNIFICANT CHANGES SERIES

Easily identify key changes from the 2003 to 2006 I-Codes®. Each title focuses on important changes in the 2006 I-Codes® that are utilized frequently, have had a change in application, or have special significance including new technologies. The straightforward analysis will help building officials, plans examiners, inspectors, contractors, design professionals, and others apply new code provisions effectively.

SIGNIFICANT CHANGES TO THE IBC® (321 PAGES)   #7024S06

SIGNIFICANT CHANGES TO THE IRC® (306 PAGES)   #7101S06

SIGNIFICANT CHANGES TO THE IPC®/ IMC®/ IFGC®
(287 PAGES)   #7202S06

SIGNIFICANT CHANGES TO THE IFC® (242 PAGES)   #7404S06

FULL-COLOR ILLUSTRATIONS! EASY TO UNDERSTAND!
BUILDING CODE BASICS: RESIDENTIAL, 2006 IRC®

ALSO AVAILABLE!

This straightforward, focused approach introduces code requirements with non-code language in an easy to read and understand format. The book covers IRC basics and corresponds to the order of construction beginning with site work and foundations, and ending with the fire and life-safety and environmental requirements of the finished building. Plumbing, mechanical, fuel gas and electrical systems are included for well-rounded coverage. Full-color illustrations help readers visualize correct code application. A glossary of code and construction terms clarifies key terminology as it applies to the code. (256 pages)

#4118S06

TO ORDER | 1-800-786-4452 | www.iccsafe.org/store

10-03677

This insert is not part of the official text of the New York State Uniform Fire Prevention and Building Code or New York State Energy Conservation Code.

3. The unit shall be provided with a separate bathroom containing a water closet, lavatory and bathtub or shower.
4. The maximum number of occupants shall be three.

404.7 Food preparation. All spaces to be occupied for food preparation purposes shall contain suitable space and equipment to store, prepare and serve foods in a sanitary manner. There shall be adequate facilities and services for the sanitary disposal of food wastes and refuse, including facilities for temporary storage.

CHAPTER 5
PLUMBING FACILITIES AND FIXTURE REQUIREMENTS

SECTION 501
GENERAL

501.1 Scope. The provisions of this chapter shall govern the minimum plumbing systems, facilities and plumbing fixtures to be provided.

501.2 Responsibility. The owner of the structure shall provide and maintain such plumbing facilities and plumbing fixtures in compliance with these requirements. A person shall not occupy as owner-occupant or permit another person to occupy any structure or premises which does not comply with the requirements of this chapter.

[P] SECTION 502
REQUIRED FACILITIES

502.1 Dwelling units. Every dwelling unit shall contain its own bathtub or shower, lavatory, water closet and kitchen sink which shall be maintained in a sanitary, safe working condition. The lavatory shall be placed in the same room as the water closet or located in close proximity to the door leading directly into the room in which such water closet is located. A kitchen sink shall not be used as a substitute for the required lavatory.

> **Exception:** Owner-occupied one-family dwellings subject to the approval of the code enforcement official.

502.2 Rooming houses. At least one water closet, lavatory and bathtub or shower shall be supplied for each four rooming units.

502.3 Hotels. Where private water closets, lavatories and baths are not provided, one water closet, one lavatory and one bathtub or shower having access from a public hallway shall be provided for each ten occupants.

502.4 Employees' facilities. A minimum of one water closet, one lavatory and one drinking facility shall be available to employees.

> **502.4.1 Drinking facilities.** Drinking facilities shall be a drinking fountain, water cooler, bottled water cooler or disposable cups next to a sink or water dispenser. Drinking facilities shall not be located in toilet rooms or bathrooms.

[P] SECTION 503
TOILET ROOMS

503.1 Privacy. Toilet rooms and bathrooms shall provide privacy and shall not constitute the only passageway to a hall or other space, or to the exterior. A door and interior locking device shall be provided for all common or shared bathrooms and toilet rooms in a multiple dwelling.

503.2 Location. Toilet rooms and bathrooms serving hotel units, rooming units or dormitory units or housekeeping units, shall have access by traversing not more than one flight of stairs and shall have access from a common hall or passageway.

503.3 Location of employee toilet facilities. Toilet facilities shall have access from within the employees' working area. The required toilet facilities shall be located not more than one story above or below the employees' working area and the path of travel to such facilities shall not exceed a distance of 500 feet (152 m). Employee facilities shall either be separate facilities or combined employee and public facilities.

> **Exception:** Facilities that are required for employees in storage structures or kiosks, which are located in adjacent structures under the same ownership, lease or control, shall not exceed a travel distance of 500 feet (152 m) from the employees' regular working area to the facilities.

503.4 Floor surface. In other than dwelling units, every toilet room floor shall be maintained to be a smooth, hard, nonabsorbent surface to permit such floor to be easily kept in a clean and sanitary condition.

[P] SECTION 504
PLUMBING SYSTEMS AND FIXTURES

504.1 General. All plumbing fixtures shall be properly installed and maintained in working order, and shall be kept free from obstructions, leaks and defects and be capable of performing the function for which such plumbing fixtures are designed. All plumbing fixtures shall be maintained in a safe, sanitary and functional condition.

504.2 Fixture clearances. Plumbing fixtures shall have adequate clearances for usage and cleaning.

504.3 Plumbing system hazards. Where it is found that a plumbing system in a structure constitutes a hazard to the occupants or the structure by reason of inadequate service, inadequate venting, cross connection, backsiphonage, improper installation, deterioration or damage or for similar reasons, the defects shall be corrected to eliminate the hazard.

SECTION 505
WATER SYSTEM

505.1 General. Every sink, lavatory, bathtub or shower, drinking fountain, water closet or other plumbing fixture shall be properly connected to either a public water system or to an approved private water system. All kitchen sinks, lavatories, laundry facilities, bathtubs and showers shall be supplied with hot or tempered and cold running water in accordance with the *Plumbing Code of New York State*.

> **Exception:** Owner-occupied one-family dwellings subject to the approval of the code enforcement official.

[P] 505.2 Contamination. The water supply shall be maintained free from contamination, and all water inlets for plumbing fixtures shall be located above the flood-level rim

PLUMBING FACILITIES AND FIXTURE REQUIREMENTS

of the fixture. Shampoo basin faucets, janitor sink faucets and other hose bibs or faucets to which hoses are attached and left in place, shall be protected by an approved atmospheric-type vacuum breaker or an approved permanently attached hose connection vacuum breaker.

505.3 Supply. The water supply system shall be installed and maintained to provide a supply of water to plumbing fixtures, devices and appurtenances in sufficient volume and at pressures adequate to enable the fixtures to function properly, safely, and free from defects and leaks.

505.4 Water heating facilities. Water heating facilities shall be properly installed, maintained and capable of providing an adequate amount of water to be drawn at every required sink, lavatory, bathtub, shower and laundry facility at a temperature of not less than 110°F (43°C) where hot water is required. A fuel-burning water heater shall not be located in any bathroom, toilet room, bedroom or other occupied room normally kept closed, unless adequate combustion air is provided. An approved combination temperature and pressure-relief valve and relief valve discharge pipe shall be properly installed and maintained on water heaters.

[P] SECTION 506
SANITARY DRAINAGE SYSTEM

506.1 General. All plumbing fixtures shall be properly connected to either a public sewer system or to an approved private sewage disposal system.

> **Exception:** Owner-occupied one-family dwellings subject to the approval of the code enforcement official.

506.2 Maintenance. Every plumbing stack, vent, waste and sewer line shall function properly and be kept free from obstructions, leaks and defects.

[P] SECTION 507
STORM DRAINAGE

507.1 General. Drainage of roofs and paved areas, yards and courts, and other open areas on the premises shall not be discharged in a manner that creates a public nuisance.

CHAPTER 6
MECHANICAL AND ELECTRICAL REQUIREMENTS

SECTION 601
GENERAL

601.1 Scope. The provisions of this chapter shall govern the minimum mechanical and electrical facilities and equipment to be provided.

601.2 Responsibility. The owner of the structure shall provide and maintain mechanical and electrical facilities and equipment in compliance with these requirements. A person shall not occupy as owner-occupant or permit another person to occupy any premises which does not comply with the requirements of this chapter.

SECTION 602
HEATING FACILITIES

602.1 Facilities required. Heating facilities shall be provided in structures as required by this section.

602.2 Residential occupancies. Dwellings shall be provided with heating facilities capable of maintaining a room temperature of 68°F (20°C) in all habitable rooms, bathrooms and toilet rooms based on the winter design dry-bulb temperature for the locality indicated in the *Energy Conservation Construction Code of New York State*. Cooking appliances shall not be used to provide space heating to meet the requirements of this section.

> **Exception:** Owner-occupied one-family dwellings subject to the approval of the code enforcement official.

602.3 Heat supply. Every owner and operator of any building who rents, leases or lets one or more dwelling unit, rooming unit, dormitory or guestroom on terms, either expressed or implied, to furnish heat to the occupants thereof shall supply heat during the period from September 15th to May 31st to maintain a temperature of not less than 68°F (20°C) in all habitable rooms, bathrooms and toilet rooms.

> **Exception:** When the outdoor temperature is below the winter outdoor design temperature for the locality, maintenance of the minimum room temperature shall not be required, provided that the heating system is operating at its full design capacity. The winter design dry-bulb temperature for the locality shall be as indicated in the *Energy Conservation Construction Code of New York State*.

602.4 Occupiable work spaces. Indoor occupiable work spaces shall be supplied with heat during the period from September 15th to May 31st to maintain a temperature of not less than 65°F (18°C) during the period the spaces are occupied.

> **Exceptions:**
> 1. Processing, storage and operation areas that require cooling or special temperature conditions.
> 2. Areas in which persons are primarily engaged in vigorous physical activities.

602.5 Occupiable public spaces. Indoor public spaces shall be supplied with heat during the period from September 15th to May 31st to maintain a temperature of not less than 68°F (20°C) in accordance with the *Building Code of New York State* during the period the spaces are occupied.

602.6 Room temperature measurement. The required room temperatures shall be measured 3 feet (914 mm) above the floor near the center of the room and 2 feet (610 mm) inward from the center of each exterior wall.

SECTION 603
MECHANICAL EQUIPMENT

603.1 Mechanical appliances. All mechanical appliances, fireplaces, solid fuel-burning appliances, cooking appliances and water heating appliances shall be properly installed and maintained in a safe working condition, and shall be capable of performing the intended function.

603.2 Removal of combustion products. All fuel-burning equipment and appliances shall be connected to an approved chimney or vent.

> **Exception:** Fuel-burning equipment and appliances which are labeled for unvented operation.

603.3 Clearances. All required clearances to combustible materials shall be maintained.

603.4 Safety controls. All safety controls for fuel-burning equipment shall be maintained in effective operation.

603.5 Combustion air. A supply of air for complete combustion of the fuel and for ventilation of the space containing the fuel-burning equipment shall be provided for the fuel-burning equipment.

603.6 Energy conservation devices. Devices intended to reduce fuel consumption by attachment to a fuel-burning appliance, to the fuel supply line thereto, or to the vent outlet or vent piping therefrom, shall not be installed unless labeled for such purpose and the installation is specifically approved.

SECTION 604
ELECTRICAL FACILITIES

604.1 Facilities required. Every occupied building shall be provided with an electrical system in compliance with the requirements of this section and Section 605.

> **Exception:** Owner-occupied one-family dwellings dwellings not supplied with electrical power, subject to the approval of the code enforcement official.

604.2 Service. The size and usage of appliances and equipment shall serve as a basis for determining the need for additional facilities in accordance with Chapter 27 of the *Building Code of New York State* or Part VIII of the *Residential Code of New York State*, as applicable.

MECHANICAL AND ELECTRICAL REQUIREMENTS

604.3 Electrical system hazards. Where it is found that the electrical system in a structure constitutes a hazard to the occupants or the structure by reason of inadequate service, improper fusing, insufficient receptacle and lighting outlets, improper wiring or installation, deterioration or damage, or for similar reasons, the defects shall be corrected to eliminate the hazard.

SECTION 605
ELECTRICAL EQUIPMENT

605.1 Installation. All electrical equipment, wiring and appliances shall be properly installed and maintained in a safe and approved manner.

605.2 Receptacles. Every habitable space in a dwelling shall contain at least two separate and remote receptacle outlets. Every laundry area shall contain at least one grounded-type receptacle or a receptacle with a ground fault circuit interrupter. Every bathroom shall contain at least one receptacle. Any new bathroom receptacle outlet shall have ground fault circuit interrupter protection.

605.3 Lighting fixtures. Every public hall, interior stairway, toilet room, kitchen, bathroom, laundry room, boiler room and furnace room shall contain at least one electric lighting fixture.

SECTION 606
ELEVATORS, ESCALATORS AND DUMBWAITERS

606.1 General. Elevators, dumbwaiters and escalators shall be maintained in compliance with ASME A17.1. The most current certificate of inspection shall be on display at all times within the elevator or attached to the escalator or dumbwaiter, or the certificate shall be available for public inspection in the office of the building operator. The inspection and tests shall be performed at not less than the periodical intervals listed in ASME A17.1, Appendix N, except where otherwise specified by the authority having jurisdiction.

606.1.1 Maintenance and inspection. Elevators, dumbwaiters, escalators and platform lifts shall be maintained and meet schedule of inspections in accord with *Building Code of New York State,* Section 3001, and Appendix N, Table-1 of ASME A17.1 and ASME A18.1.

606.2 Elevators. In buildings equipped with passenger elevators, at least one elevator shall be maintained in operation at all times when the building is occupied.

Exception: Buildings equipped with only one elevator shall be permitted to have the elevator temporarily out of service for testing or servicing.

SECTION 607
DUCT SYSTEMS

607.1 General. Duct systems shall be maintained free of obstructions and shall be capable of performing the required function.

SECTION 608
ASSISTIVE LISTENING SYSTEMS

608.1 General. The owner or operator of each assembly space shall have the assistive listening system and all components thereof inspected annually and shall thereupon certify to the local authority having jurisdiction that each such system continues to comply with the *Building Code of New York State, Appendix L,* including the minimum number of required receivers/transducers.

CHAPTER 7
FIRE SAFETY REQUIREMENTS

SECTION 701
GENERAL

701.1 Scope. The provisions of this chapter shall govern the minimum conditions and standards for fire safety relating to structures and exterior premises, including fire safety facilities and equipment to be provided.

701.2 Responsibility. The owner of the premises shall provide and maintain such fire safety facilities and equipment in compliance with these requirements. A person shall not occupy as owner-occupant or permit another person to occupy any premises that do not comply with the requirements of this chapter.

[F] SECTION 702
MEANS OF EGRESS

702.1 General. A safe, continuous and unobstructed path of travel shall be provided from any point in a building or structure to the public way. Means of egress shall comply with the *Fire Code of New York State*.

702.2 Aisles. The required width of aisles in accordance with the *Fire Code of New York State* shall be unobstructed.

702.3 Locked doors. All means of egress doors shall be readily openable from the side from which egress is to be made without the need for keys, special knowledge or effort, except where the door hardware conforms to that permitted by the *Fire Code of New York State*.

702.4 Emergency escape openings. Required emergency escape openings shall be maintained in accordance with the code in effect at the time of construction, and the following. Required emergency escape and rescue openings shall be operational from the inside of the room without the use of keys or tools. Bars, grilles, grates or similar devices are permitted to be placed over emergency escape and rescue openings, provided the minimum net clear opening size complies with the code that was in effect at the time of construction and such devices shall be releasable or removable from the inside without the use of a key, tool or force greater than that which is required for normal operation of the escape and rescue opening.

[F] SECTION 703
FIRE-RESISTANCE RATINGS

703.1 Fire-resistance-rated assemblies. The required fire-resistance rating of fire-resistance-rated walls, fire stops, shaft enclosures, partitions and floors shall be maintained.

703.2 Opening protectives. Required opening protectives shall be maintained in an operative condition. All fire and smokestop doors shall be maintained in operable condition. Fire doors and smoke barrier doors shall not be blocked or obstructed or otherwise made inoperable.

[F] SECTION 704
FIRE PROTECTION SYSTEMS

704.1 General. All systems, devices and equipment to detect a fire, actuate an alarm, or suppress or control a fire or any combination thereof shall be maintained in an operable condition at all times in accordance with the *Fire Code of New York State*.

704.2 Smoke alarms. Single- or multiple-station smoke alarms shall be installed and maintained in Groups R-2, R-3, and R-4 and in dwellings regulated by the *Residential Code of New York State*, regardless of occupant load at all of the following locations:

1. On the ceiling or wall outside of each separate sleeping area in the immediate vicinity of bedrooms.

2. In each room used for sleeping purposes.

3. In each story within a dwelling unit, including basements but not including crawl spaces and uninhabitable attics. In dwellings or dwelling units with split levels and without an intervening door between the adjacent levels, a smoke alarm installed on the upper level shall suffice for the adjacent lower level provided that the lower level is less than one full story below the upper level.

Single- or multiple-station smoke alarms shall be installed in other groups, including Group R-1 and I-1, in accordance with the *Fire Code of New York State*.

> **Exception:** Group R-2 occupancies used as dormitories, fraternities, sororities and similar student housing and meeting the requirements of the *Fire Code of New York State*, Section 907.2.9.1.

704.3 Power source. In Group R occupancies and in dwellings not regulated as Group R occupancies, single-station smoke alarms shall receive their primary power from the building wiring, provided that such wiring is served from a commercial source, or an on-site electrical power system, and shall be equipped with a battery backup. Smoke alarms shall emit a signal when the batteries are low. Wiring shall be permanent and without a disconnecting switch other than as required for overcurrent protection.

> **Exception:** Smoke alarms are permitted to be solely battery operated in buildings where no construction is taking place, buildings that are not served from a commercial power source, or an on-site electrical power system, and in existing areas of buildings undergoing alterations or repairs that do not result in the removal of interior wall or ceiling finishes.

704.4 Interconnection. Where more than one smoke alarm is required to be installed within an individual dwelling unit in Group R occupancies and in dwellings not regulated as Group R occupancies, the smoke alarms shall be intercon-

FIRE SAFETY REQUIREMENTS

nected in such a manner that the activation of one alarm will activate all of the alarms in the individual unit. The alarm shall be clearly audible in all bedrooms over background noise levels with all intervening doors closed.

Exceptions:

1. Interconnection is not required in buildings which are not undergoing alterations, repairs, or construction of any kind.

2. Smoke alarms in existing areas are not required to be interconnected where alterations or repairs do not result in the removal of interior wall or ceiling finishes exposing the structure.

3. Smoke alarms shall not be required to be interconnected where battery-operated alarms are permitted.

SECTION 705
CARBON MONOXIDE ALARMS

705.1 General. Carbon monoxide alarms and detectors shall comply with the *Fire Code of New York State*.

CHAPTER 8
REFERENCED STANDARDS

SECTION 801

This chapter lists the standards that are referenced in various sections of this document. The standards are listed herein by the promulgating agency of the standard, the standard identification, the effective date and title and the section or sections of this document that reference the standard. The application of the referenced standards shall be as specified in Section 102.5.

* Denotes standards that are incorporated by reference into 19 NYCRR Part 1226.

Margin markings have not been made in this chapter. The date of the reference standard will denote the new standards from the 2007 code.

ASME
American Society of Mechanical Engineers
Three Park Avenue
New York, NY 10016-5990

Standard reference number	Title	Referenced in code section number
*A17.1—04	Safety Code for Elevators and Escalators	606.1.1
*A18.1—05	Safety Standard for Platform Lifts and Stairway Chairlifts	606.1.1

ASTM
ASTM International
100 Barr Harbor Drive
West Conshohocken, PA 19428-2959

Standard reference number	Title	Referenced in code section number
*F1346—91 (1996)	Performance Specifications for Safety Covers and Labeling Requirements for All Covers for Swimming Pools, Spas and Hot Tubs	303.2, 303.7
F2208—08	Standard Safety Specification for Residential Pool Alarms	303.6

EPA
United States Environmental Protection Agency
Ariel Rios Building
1200 Pennsylvania Avenue, N.W.
Washington, DC 20460

Standard reference number	Title	Referenced in code section number
40 CFR 745—(2008)	Lead-Based Paint Poisoning Prevention in Certain Residential Structures	304.2, 305.3

ICC
International Code Council
5203 Leesburg Pike, Suite 600
Falls Church, VA 22041-3401

Standard reference number	Title	Referenced in code section number
BCNYS—10	Building Code of New York State	4.2, 105.1, 201.3, 302.3.1, 303.3, 306.1, 401.3, 602.5, 604.2, 606.1, 608, 702.3
EBCNYS—10	Existing Building Code of New York State	102.3, 102.6, 102.8, 103.2, 201.3

REFERENCED STANDARDS

ICC—continued

Standard reference number	Title	Referenced in code section number
ECCCNYS—10	Energy Conservation Construction Code of New York State	602.2, 602.3
FCNYS—10	Fire Code of New York State	103.4, 105.1, 107.2, 201.3, 609.1, 702.1, 702.2, 702.3, 704.1, 704.2
FGCNYS—10	Fuel Gas Code of New York State	102.6, 103.2, 201.3
MCNYS—10	Mechanical Code of New York State	201.3
PCNYS—10	Plumbing Code of New York State	201.3, 505.1, 602.2, 602.3
RCNYS—10	Residential Code of New York State	401.3, 402.2, 404.3

NFPA

National Fire Protection Association
1 Batterymarch Park
Quincy, MA 02169-7471

Standard reference number	Title	Referenced in code section number
720—09	Standard for the Installation of Carbon Monoxide (CO) Detection and Warning Equipment	705

INDEX

A

ACCEPTED ENGINEERING METHODS 104.2

ACCESS
Egress 702
From bedrooms 404.4.2
Plumbing fixtures, access for cleaning 504.2
To public way 702.1
Toilet room as passageway 503.1
Water closet 404.4.3

ADJACENT
Privacy (hotel units, rooming units) 404.1

ADMINISTRATION
Scope 101.2

AGENT (See also OPERATOR, OWNER) 202

AIR
Combustion air 603.5

AISLES
Minimum width 702.2

ALTERATION
Applicability of other codes 102.3
Condemnation 108.1, 108.2
Inspection 104.3
Prosecution 106.3
Unlawful acts 106.1

ANCHOR
Architectural trim 304.8
Signs, marquees and awnings 304.9

APPLIANCE
Cooking 403.3, 602.2
Heating 602.2, 603.1
Mechanical 603.1

APPLICATION
Other codes 102.6

APPROVAL
Alternatives 105.2
Authority 104.1, 105.2
Modifications 105.1

APPROVED
Alternative materials, methods and
 equipment 103.3
Definition 202
Energy conservation devices 603.6
Fireplaces 603.1
Garbage storage facilities 307.3.1
Used materials and equipment 103.2

ARCHITECTURAL
Structural members 304.4
Trim 304.8

ARTIFICIAL
Lighting of habitable rooms 401.3
Lighting of other spaces 402.3

AUTOMOBILE
Motor vehicles 302.8

AWNING
Signs, marquees and awnings 304.9

B

BALCONY
Handrails and guardrails 306.1

BASEMENT
Definition 202
Hatchways 304.16
Windows 304.17

BATHROOM
Common bathrooms 502.3, 503.1
Hotels 502.3
Lighting 605.3
Locks 503.1
Outlets required 605.2
Privacy 503.1
Ventilation 403.2

BATHTUB
Required facilities 502.1
Rooming houses 502.2
Sewage system 506.1
Water heating facilities 505.4
Water system 505.1

BOILER
Unsafe equipment 107.1.2

C

CAPACITY
Heating facilities 602.2, 602.3, 602.4

CAR (See AUTOMOBILE)

CARBON MONOXIDE ALARMS 705

CEILING
Basement rooms 404.3
Fire-resistance ratings 703.1

INDEX

    Interior surfaces 305.3
    Minimum height 404.3

CHANGE, MODIFY
    Application of other codes 102.2

CHIMNEY
    Exterior structure 304.11
    Fireplaces. 603.1
    Flue 603.2, 603.3

CLEANING
    Access for cleaning 504.2
    Bathroom and kitchen floors 305.3, 503.4
    Disposal of garbage. .307.3
    Disposal of rubbish. 307.2
    Interior sanitation 307.1
    Interior surfaces 305.3
    Occupant 305.1
    Plumbing facilities, maintained. 504.1
    Required plumbing facilities. 502
    Responsibility of persons. 305.1
    Trash containers 307.3.2
    Vacant structures and land 301.3

CLEARANCE
    Heating facilities. 603.3
    Plumbing fixtures 504.2

CLOSING
    Vacant structures 107.2

CLOTHES DRYER
    Exhaust 403.5

CODE ENFORCEMENT OFFICIAL
    Condemnation 108.1
    Placarding 107.3
    Removal of placard 107.5
    Vacant structures 107.2

COLD WATER
    Drinking 502.4.1
    Required facilities. 502
    Rooming houses 502.2
    Water system 505

COMBUSTION
    Combustion air. 603.5

CONDEMNATION
    Closing of vacant structures. 107.2
    Placarding 107
    Removal of placard 107.5

CONNECTION
    Plumbing fixtures 504.1
    Sewage system 506.1
    Water heating. 505.4
    Water system 505.1

CONTAINER
    Garbage 307.3.2

    Rubbish storage 307.2.1

CONTINUOUS
    Egress. 703.1

CONTROL
    Insect and rat control 302.5, 304.5, 307.1
    Safety controls 603.4

COOLING
    Cooling towers 304.11

CORRIDOR
    Accumulation of rubbish 307.1
    Light 402.2
    Lighting fixtures. 605.3
    Ratings maintained. 703
    Toilet rooms, access. 503.1

D

DAMP, DAMPNESS
    Roofs. 304.7
    Window, door frames 304.13

DANGEROUS, HAZARDOUS
    Condemnation 107.1
    Electrical hazards 604.3
    Elevators. 606.1
    Fire safety 701.1
    Heating facilities 602, 603.1
    Imminent danger. 202
    Unsafe structures and
        equipment 107.1.1, 107.1.2

DECKS
    Handrails and guardrails. 304.12
    Maintenance .304.2, 304.10

DECORATION
    Exterior structure 304.8

DETECTORS
    Smoke. 704

DETERIORATION
    Exterior walls. 304.6

DIRECT
    Egress. 703.1

DISPOSAL
    Disposal of garbage 307.3
    Disposal of rubbish 307.2

DOOR
    Exit doors 702.3
    Fire 703.2
    Hardware 304.15
    Interior surfaces 305.3
    Locks. 304.15, 702.3
    Maintenance .304.13, 304.15

Weather tight 304.13
Window and door frames 304.13

DORMITORY (see also ROOMING HOUSES, HOTELS, MOTEL)
Locked doors 702.3
Privacy 503.1, 503.2

DRAIN, DRAINAGE
Basement hatchways 304.16
Plumbing connections 506
Storm drainage......................... 507

DUCT
Exhaust duct.......................... 304.9

DUST
Process ventilation 403.4

DWELLING
Cleanliness.................... 305.1, 307.1
Definition............................202
Electrical 604.1
Heating facilities 602
Required facilities 502

E

EASEMENT
Definition............................202

EGRESS
Aisles 702.2
Emergency escape..................... 702.4
General.............................. 702.1
Lighting 402.2
Locked doors 702.3
Obstructions prohibited................ 702.1
Stairs, porches and
railings................ 304.10, 305.5, 306.1

ELECTRIC, ELECTRICAL
Condemnation 107.1
Facilities required 604.1
General............................. 601.1
Hazards 604.3
Installation........................... 605.1
Luminaires 605.3
Receptacles 604.3, 605.2
Responsibility 601.2
Service 604.2

ELEVATOR
Condemnation 107.1
General............................ 606.1
Maintenance................... 606.1, 606.2

EMERGENCY
Emergency measures 108

Emergency orders..................... 107.3
Escape............................... 702.4

ENFORCEMENT
Scope 101.2

EQUIPMENT
Alternative 103.3
Combustion air 603.5
Condemnation.............. 107.1, 107.3
Electrical installation 605.1
Emergency order..................... 108
Energy conservation devices 603.6
Fire safety requirements, responsibility 701.2
Flue 603.2
Installation 603.1
Interior structure 305.1
Placarding 107.3, 107.4
Prohibited occupancy 107.4
Responsibility 601.2
Safety controls....................... 603.4
Scope 101.2
Scope, mechanical and electrical 601.1
Unsafe............... 107.1.1, 107.1.2, 108
Used 103.2

EXHAUST
Clothes dryer........................ 403.5
Exhaust ducts 304.9
Process ventilation 403.4

EXISTING
Remedies 102.2
Scope 101.2
Structural members................... 304.4
Structures 101.3

EXTERIOR
Decorative features................... 304.8
Egress.............................. 702.1
Exterior structure...................... 304
Exterior walls........................ 304.6
Painting 304.2, 304.6
Rodent harborage 302.5, 304.5
Sanitation........................... 303.1
Scope 301.1
Stair............................... 304.10
Street numbers 304.3
Weather tight........................ 304.13

EXTERMINATE
Definition........................... 202
Insect and rodent control 302.5, 303.14, 304.5
Responsibility of owner 301.2, 308.2
Responsibility of tenant-
occupant 301.2, 307.3, 308.5

F

FAN
    Exhaust vents...........................302.6

FENCE
    Accessory..............................302.7
    Maintenance...........................304.2

FIRE
    Fire-resistance ratings..................703.1
    General, fire-protection systems...........704
    Responsibility, fire safety...............701.2
    Scope..................................101.2
    Scope, fire safety......................701.1
    Smoke alarms.........................704.1

FLAMMABLE LIQUID
    Containers............................107.1.2

FLOOR, FLOORING
    Area for bedrooms and living rooms........404.5
    Fire-resistance ratings..................703.1
    Interior surfaces................305.1, 305.3
    Space requirements............404.5, 404.6

FOOD PREPARATION
    Cooking equipment................403.3, 602.2
    Sanitary condition...............305.1, 404.7
    Ventilation.............................403.4

FOUNDATION
    Condemnation........................107.1.1
    Foundation walls......................304.5

FRAME
    Window and door frames................304.13

G

GAS
    Energy conservation devices.............603.6
    Exhaust vents..........................302.6
    Process ventilation.....................403.4

GLAZING
    Materials............................304.13.1

GRADE
    Drainage.........................302.2, 507

GUARD
    Basement windows.....................304.17
    Definition..............................202
    Anchorage and maintenance.............304.12

H

HABITABLE
    Definition..............................202
    Light..................................402
    Minimum ceiling height..................404.3
    Minimum room width....................404.2
    Required plumbing facilities..............502
    Residential heating facilities...602.2, 602.3, 602.4
    Space requirements....................404.5
    Ventilation.............................403

HANDRAIL
    Handrails................304.12, 305.6, 306.1

HARDWARE
    Door hardware..................304.15, 702.3
    Openable windows....................304.13.2

HAZARDOUS (See DANGEROUS, HAZARDOUS)

HEAT, HEATING
    Cooking equipment................403.3, 602.2
    Energy conservation devices.............603.6
    Fireplaces............................603.1
    Heating..............................603.1
    Mechanical equipment..................603.1
    Required capabilities....................602
    Residential heating................602.2, 602.3
    Scope.................................101.2
    Supply...............................602.3
    Water heating facilities..................505.4
    Water system..........................505

HOUSEKEEPING UNIT
    Definition..............................202

HEIGHT
    Minimum ceiling height..................404.3

HOT (See HEAT, HEATING)

HOTELS, ROOMING HOUSES AND DORMITORY UNITS, MOTELS
    Definition..............................202
    Locked doors.........................702.3
    Required facilities......................502
    Toilet rooms..........................503

I

INFESTATION
    Condemnation........................107.1.3
    Definition..............................202
    Insect and rodent...............302.5, 308.1

INSECTS
    Extermination..........................308
    Infestation............................308.1

INTENT
    Code.................................101.3
    Rule-making authority....................102

INTERIOR
    Interior structure.......................305
    Interior surfaces.......................305.3

INDEX

Means of egress..........................702
Sanitation.............................305.1

K

KITCHEN
Electrical outlets required................605.2
Minimum width.........................404.2
Prohibited use..........................404.4.4
Room lighting..........................605.3
Water heating facilities..................505.4

L

LANDING
Handrails and guards............304.12, 305.4, 305.5, 306.1
Maintenance..............304.10, 305.5, 305.6

LAUNDRY
Room lighting..........................605.3
Water heating facilities..................505.4

LAVATORY
Hotels................................502.3
Required facilities........................502
Rooming houses........................502.2
Sanitary drainage system..................506
Water heating facilities..................505.4
Water system...........................505

LEAD PAINT......................304.2, 305.3

LEASE (SELL, RENT)
Heat supplied..........................602.3

LIGHT, LIGHTING
Common halls and stairways........402.2, 605.3
Luminaires............................605.3
General................................402
Habitable rooms........................402.1
Other spaces...........................402.3
Responsibility..........................401.2
Scope.................................101.2
Toilet rooms...........................605.3

LIVING ROOM
Room area.............................404.5

LOAD, LOADING
Elevators, escalators and dumbwaiters.....606.1
Handrails and guards....................304.12
Live load..........................304.4, 305.2
Stairs and porches.................304.10, 305.2
Structural members................304.4, 305.2

M

MAINTENANCE
Required..............................102.2

MATERIAL
Alternative............................103.3
Used..................................103.2

MEANS OF EGRESS (See EGRESS)

MECHANICAL
Installation............................603.1
Responsibility..........................601.2
Scope.................................601.1
Ventilation, general.......................403
Ventilation, toilet rooms..................403.2

MINIMUM
Ceiling height..........................404.3
Room width...........................404.2
Scope.................................301.1

MODIFICATION
Approval..............................105.1

MOTEL (See HOTELS)

MOTOR VEHICLES
Inoperative............................302.8
Painting...............................302.8

N

NATURAL
Lighting..........................401.3, 402
Ventilation........................401.3, 403

NOTICE
Appeal................................109.3
Form..................................109.3
Method of service.......................109.3
Owner, responsible person..........101.2, 301
Placarding of structure....................108
Vacating structure...................107.4, 108

NOXIOUS
Process ventilation......................403.4
Weeds................................302.4

NUISANCE
Closing of vacant structures...............107.1

O

OBSTRUCTION
Light..................................402.1

OCCUPANCY (See USE)

INDEX

OPENABLE
  Definition 202
  Habitable rooms. 403.1
  Locked doors 702.3
  Windows. 304.13.2

OPERATOR
  Definition 202

ORDER (See NOTICE)

ORDINANCE, RULE
  Applicability 102.1
  Application for appeal 109.3

OUTLET
  Electrical. 605.2

OWNER
  Closing of vacant structures. 107.2
  Definition 202
  Extermination. 308
  Failure to comply 109.1
  Insect and rodent control 302.5, 308.2, 308.4
  Notice. 109
  Placarding of structure. 107
  Responsibility. 301.2
  Responsibility, fire safety 701.2
  Responsibility, light, ventilation 401.2
  Responsibility, mechanical and electrical 601.2
  Responsibility, plumbing facilities 501.2
  Right of entry 109
  Rubbish storage. 307.2.1
  Scope. 101.2

P

PASSAGEWAY
  Common hall and stairway 402.2
  Interior surfaces .305.3
  Toilet rooms, direct access 503.1

PENALTY
  Placarding of structure. 107
  Prohibited occupancy. 107.4
  Removal of placard 107.5
  Scope. 101.2
  Violations 109.1

PEST (see also VERMIN)
  Condemnation 107.1
  Extermination. 308.1
  Insect and rodent control 302.5, 308.1

PLACARD, POST
  Closing 107.1.1, 107.1.3
  Condemnation 107.1
  Notice. 107.3
  Placarding of structure. 107.3, 107.4, 107.5
  Prohibited use 107.4
  Removal. 107.5

PLUMBING
  Access 504.2
  Clean and sanitary 504.1
  Connections 505.1
  Contamination. 505.2
  Employees' facilities 503.3
  Fixtures 504.1
  Required facilities 502
  Responsibility 501.2
  Sanitary drainage system. 506
  Scope 501.1
  Storm drainage 507
  Supply. 505.3
  Water heating facilities 505.4

PORCH
  Handrails. 304.12, 305.5, 306.1
  Structurally sound 304.10

PORTABLE (TEMPORARY)
  Cooking equipment. 603.1

PRESSURE
  Water supply. 505.3

PRIVATE, PRIVACY
  Bathtub or shower. 503.1
  Occupancy limitations. 404.1
  Required plumbing facilities 502
  Sewage system 506.1
  Water closet and lavatory 503.1
  Water system 505.1

PROPERTY, PREMISES
  Cleanliness 304.1, 307.1
  Condemnation 107.1
  Definition. 202
  Emergency measures. 108
  Exterior areas 302
  Extermination, multiple occupancy. . . .302.5, 308.4
  Extermination, single occupancy 302.5, 308.3
  Failure to comply 109.1
  Grading and drainage. 302.2
  Responsibility 301.2
  Scope 301.1
  Storm drainage 507
  Vacant structures and land. 301.3

PROTECTION
  Basement windows. 304.17
  Fire-protection systems 704
  Signs, marquees and awnings 304.9

PUBLIC
  Cleanliness 304.1, 305.1
  Egress. 702.1
  Hallway 502.3
  Sewage system 506.1
  Toilet rooms 503
  Vacant structures and land. 301.3
  Water system 505

INDEX

PUBLIC WAY
Definition.................................202

R

RAIN
Basement hatchways....................304.16
Exterior walls..........................304.6
Grading and drainage....................302.2
Roofs..................................304.7
Window and door frames................304.13

REPAIR
Application of other codes..............102.2
Chimneys..............................304.11
Exterior surfaces......................304.1
Maintenance............................102.2
Public areas...........................302.3
Signs, marquees and awnings............304.9
Stairs and porches....................304.10
Weather tight.........................304.13
Workmanship............................103.5

RESIDENTIAL
Extermination...........................308
Residential heating....................602.2
Scope..................................101.2

RESPONSIBILITY
Extermination...........................308
Fire safety............................701.2
Garbage disposal.......................307.3
General................................301.2
Mechanical and electrical..............601.2
Persons................................301.1
Placarding of structure.........107.3, 108.4
Plumbing facilities....................501.2
Rubbish storage......................307.2.1
Scope............................101.2, 301.1

REVOKE, REMOVE
Existing remedies......................109.1
Process ventilation....................403.4
Removal of placard.....................107.5
Rubbish removal......................307.2.1

RIGHT OF ENTRY
Duties and powers of code official.....109.1
Inspections............................109.1

RODENTS
Basement hatchways....................304.16
Condemnation............................107
Exterior surfaces......................304.6
Extermination....................302.5, 308
Guards for basement windows...........304.17
Harborage..............................302.5
Insect and rodent control..............308.1

ROOF
Exterior structure....................304.1
Roofs.................................304.7
Storm drainage.........................507

ROOM
Bedroom and living room........404.4, 404.5.2
Cooking facilities.....................403.3
Direct access..........................503.2
Habitable.......................402.1, 403.1
Heating facilities.....................602
Light..................................402
Minimum ceiling heights................404.3
Minimum occupancy area requirements....404.5
Minimum width..........................404.2
Overcrowding...........................404.5
Prohibited use.......................404.4.4
Temperature.............602.3, 602.4, 602.5
Toilet.................................503
Ventilation............................403

ROOMING HOUSES (See DORMITORY)

RUBBISH
Accumulation...........................307.1
Definition.............................202
Disposal...............................307.2
Garbage facilities...................307.3.1
Rubbish storage......................307.2.1
Storage..............................307.2.1

S

SAFETY, SAFE
Chimney...............................304.11
Condemnation...........................107.1
Electrical installation................605.1
Emergency measures.....................108
Fire safety requirements...............701
Fireplaces.............................603.1
Intent.................................101.3
Safety controls........................603.4
Scope..................................101.2
Unsafe structures and equipment......107.1.1

SANITARY
Bathroom and kitchen floors............305.3
Cleanliness.....................304.1, 305.1
Disposal of garbage....................307.3
Disposal of rubbish....................307.2
Exterior property areas................302.1
Exterior structure....................304.1
Food preparation.......................404.7
Furnished by occupant..................302.1
Interior surfaces.....................304.3
Plumbing fixtures......................504.1
Required plumbing facilities...........502
Scope..................................101.2

INDEX

SASH
Window 304.13

SEPARATION
Fire-resistance ratings 703
Privacy 404.1
Separation of units 404.1
Water closet and lavatory 502.1

SERVICE
Electrical 604.2
Service on occupant 107.3

SEWER
General 506.1
Maintenance 506.2

SHOWER
Bathtub or shower 502.1
Rooming houses 502.2
Water heating facilities 505.4
Water system 505

SIGN
Signs, marquees and awnings 304.9

SINGLE-FAMILY DWELLING
Extermination 308.3

SINK
Kitchen sink 502.1
Sewage system 506
Water supply 505.3

SIZE
Habitable room, light 402
Habitable room, ventilation 403
Room area .... Table 404.5

SLEEPING
Area for sleeping purposes 404.4.1
Cooking facilities 403.3

SMOKE
Alarms 704.2
Interconnection 704.4
Power source 704.3

SPACE
General, light 402
General, ventilation 403
Occupancy limitations 404
Privacy 404.1
Scope 401.1

STACK
Chimneys 304.11

STAIRS
Common halls and stairways, light 402.2
Exit facilities 305.4, 305.5
Handrails 304.12, 305.5
Luminaires 605.3
Public areas 302.3
Stairs and porches 304.10

STANDARD
Referenced 102.5

STORAGE
Food preparation 404.7
Garbage storage facilities 307.3
Rubbish storage facilities 307.2.1
Sanitation 307.1

STRUCTURE
Accessory structures 302.7
Closing of vacant structures 107.2
Definition 202
Emergency measures 108
General, exterior 304.1
General, condemnation 107.1
General, interior structure 305.1
Placarding of structure 107
Scope 301.1
Structural members 304.4, 305.2
Vacant structures and land 301.3

SUPPLY
Combustion air 603.5
Connections 505.1
Water heating facilities 505.4
Water supply 505.3
Water system 505

SURFACE
Exterior surfaces 304.2, 304.6
Interior surfaces 305.3

SWIMMING
Swimming pools 303.1, 303.2
Safety covers 303.2

T

TEMPERATURE
Nonresidential structures 602.4
Residential buildings 602.2
Water heating facilities 505.4

TENANT
Scope 101.2, 202

TOXIC
Process ventilation 403.4

TRASH
Rubbish and garbage 307

U

UNOBSTRUCTED
Access to public way 702.1
General, egress 702.1

UNSAFE
Equipment...........................107.1.2
Existing remedies......................109.1
General, condemnation..................107
Notices and orders.....................109.1
Structure............................107.1.1

USE
Application of other codes..............102.6

V

VACANT
Closing of vacant structures............107.2
Emergency measure.....................108.1
Placarding of structure..................107
Vacant structures and land..............301.3

VAPOR
Exhaust vents........................302.6
Process ventilation....................403.4

VEHICLES
Inoperative..........................302.8
Painting.............................302.8

VENT
Connections..........................504.3
Exhaust vents........................302.6
Flue.................................603.2

VENTILATION
Clothes dryer exhaust..................403.5
Combustion air.......................603.5
Definition.............................202
General, ventilation....................403
Habitable rooms......................403.1
Process ventilation....................403.4
Recirculation...................403.2, 403.4
Toilet rooms.........................403.2

VERMIN
Condemnation...................107.1.3, 108
Insect and rodent control...........302.5, 308

VIOLATION
Condemnation..........................107
General...............................107
Notice..........................107, 107.3
Placarding of structure......107.3, 107.5, 108.4

W

WALK
Sidewalks............................302.3

WALL
Accessory structures...................302.7
Exterior surfaces.................304.2, 304.6
Exterior walls........................304.6
Foundation walls.....................304.5

General, fire-resistance rating............703.1
Interior surfaces.......................305.3
Outlets required.......................605.2
Temperature measurement..............602.6

WASTE
Disposal of garbage....................307.3
Disposal of rubbish....................307.2
Dwelling units........................502.1
Garbage storage facilities..............307.3.1

WATER
Basement hatchways..................304.16
Connections..........................506.1
Contamination.......................505.2
General, sewage........................506
General, storm drainage.................507
General, water system..................505
Heating.............................505.4
Hotels..............................502.3
Kitchen sink.........................502.1
Required facilities.....................502
Rooming houses......................502.2
Supply..............................505.3
System...............................505
Toilet rooms..........................503
Water heating facilities................505.4

WEATHER, CLIMATE
Heating facilities......................602
Rule-making authority..................109.1

WEATHERSTRIP
Window and door frames..............304.13

WEEDS
Noxious weeds.......................302.4

WIDTH
Minimum room width..................404.2

WIND
Weather tight........................304.13
Window and door frames..............304.13

WINDOW
Emergency escape....................702.4
Glazing............................304.13.1
Guards for basement windows...........304.17
Habitable rooms......................402.1
Interior surface.......................305.3
Light.................................402
Openable windows..................304.13.2
Toilet rooms.........................403.2
Ventilation............................403
Weather tight........................304.13
Window and door frames..............304.13

WORKER
Employee facilities...............503.3, 602.4

WORKMANSHIP
General.............................103.5

For Reference

Not to be taken from this room